Practice Tests Key Stage 2
Science

John Aldridge

Sheila Dampney

Oxford University Press

Acknowledgements
Many thanks to the editorial team at Aldridge Press: Charlotte Rolfe, Sarah Henderson, Felix Muriithi, Sheila Dampney, Jocelyne and David.

Oxford University Press
Great Clarendon Street, Oxford OX2 6DP

Oxford New York
Athens Auckland Bangkok Bogota Bombay
Buenos Aires Calcutta Cape Town Dar es Salaam
Delhi Florence Hong Kong Istanbul Karachi
Kuala Lumpur Madras Madrid Melbourne
Mexico City Nairobi Paris Singapore
Taipei Tokyo Toronto Warsaw

and associated companies in
Berlin Ibadan

Oxford is a trade mark of Oxford University Press

© John Aldridge and Sheila Dampney 1996

First published 1996
Reprinted 1997

ISBN 0 19 838196 4

Designed by Geoffrey Wadsley
Illustrations by Barking Dog Art
Packaged by Aldridge Press

Printed in Hong Kong

All rights reserved. No part of this publication may be reproduced, stored in a retrieval system, or transmitted, in any form or by any means, without the prior permission in writing of Oxford University Press. Within the U.K., exceptions are allowed in respect of any fair dealing for the purpose of research or private study, or criticism or review, as permitted under the Copyright, Designs and Patents Act, 1988, or in the case of reprographic reproduction in accordance with the terms of licences issued by the Copyright Licensing Agency. Enquiries concerning reproduction outside those terms and in other countries should be sent to the Rights Department, Oxford University Press, at the address above.

Contents

Using this book		4
Test 1	Levels 3 and 4	6
Test 2	Levels 3 and 4	13
Test 3	Levels 3 to 5	20
Test 4	Levels 3 to 5	26
Test 5	Levels 3 to 5	33
Test 6	Levels 4 and 5	41
Test 7	Levels 5 and 6	48
Answers		55
National Curriculum record		62
Pupil achievement record		64

Using this book

What are the Key Stage 2 Tests?

- In England, Wales and Northern Ireland all pupils aged between 10 and 11 must take a National Test in three subjects: English, Mathematics and Science. The results of these tests will be reported to parents and passed on to the next school.

- The National Curriculum is divided into Levels matched to ability. Level 1 is the starting point for children aged 5, and Level 10 for very able 16-year-olds. The average level reached by an 11-year-old child should be Level 4, although a few very able children will reach Level 6. Most children will be working on Levels 4 and 5 when they are in Year 6 and aged 10 to 11.

- The National Curriculum tests for science taken by children in school cover Levels 3 to 5 with a special Level 6 test taken by the most able.

How can this book help?

- This book has been designed for children aged 10–11, to help them prepare before being assessed by the national tests. The questions in each test will give valuable practice for these National Curriculum tests and will give you information about how well your child is getting on with National Curriculum science.

- The tests cover Levels 3 to 6 of the National Curriculum with particular emphasis on Levels 4 and 5.

- The science work being tested in this book covers three broad content areas:
    Life processes and living things
    Materials and their properties
    Physical processes.
  It matches what is covered in the national tests.

- The chart on pages 62 and 63 shows how each question relates to each of these three science areas. It can also be used to show where your child needs more help.

Using this book

- There are 7 tests in this book. Each test should take your child about 30 minutes to complete, but don't rush or pressurize them. Encourage them to do as much as possible but allow them to stop when they want to – remember that these are only practice tests.
- You can give some help to your child if they seem unsure as to what to do, provided this help does not extend to giving the answer or showing them how

USING THIS BOOK

to reach the answer. The help should be confined to encouraging and reassuring them and confirming what they have to do.

Materials needed

- pencil, rubber and a centimetre ruler.

Instructions to your child

- Write the start and finish times on the test and encourage your child to work swiftly but carefully through the test.
- Read all the questions very carefully. Look at the pictures and diagrams because they are part of the test.
- The main parts of all the questions are in coloured boxes and the pencil shows where to write your answer.
- The questions get more difficult as you work through each test. Try all the questions but if you can't do one don't worry, just move on to the next question. At the end of the test go back, check your answers and have another go at any questions you found difficult the first time.

Marking the tests

- The answers are on pages 55 to 61.
- At the end of each set of answers is a guide to the science level your child has achieved in that test.
- Encourage and reassure your child: confidence is an important factor when sitting for any test.

Finding your child's level

- An approximate level is found at the end of the answers to each test, and this gives an indication of how your child has done. A more accurate assessment can be obtained by adding the results of all the tests on the Pupil Achievement Record (page 64).
- This overall calculation will indicate whether your child has achieved Level 3, 4 or 5 of the National Curriculum in these tests. For very able children it will show whether they are beginning to work at Level 6.
- It is important to remember that science at Levels 4 and 5 is quite demanding for children aged 10 to 11 and that the national average is about Level 4. Any child reaching Level 5 is doing very well indeed.
- Use the chart on pages 62/3 as a guide to giving your child extra help. The chart shows both the level and the science topic being assessed.

Teacher assessment

Not all the science work covered in schools as part of the National Curriculum is tested through pencil and paper tests. Much of this is based on practical activities done in the classroom. Teachers will use their experience and expertise to assess your child in these areas and add this information to the test results to give a final science level for your child.

TEST 1   LEVELS 3 to 4

• Test 1 •

Time started :
Time finished :

Living things

1

snail   thrush   lettuce

Snails eat lettuce.
Thrushes eat snails.

(a) Write this as a food chain.

Snail eats lettuce Thrush eats snail

(b) Name the **predator** in this food chain.

~~thrust~~ thrush

2 Choose **four** of these words to label the parts of a flower correctly.

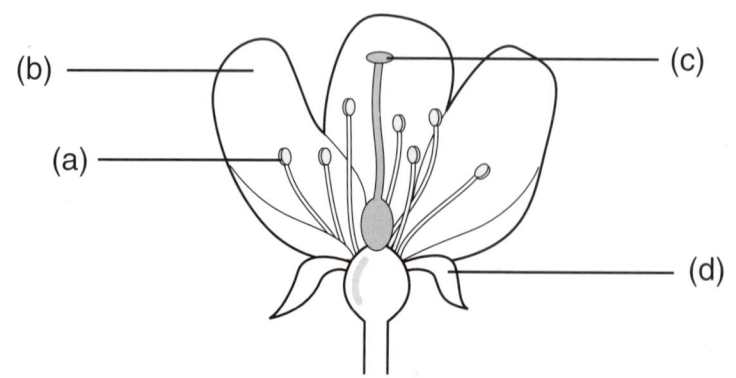

(b) ——
(a) ——
(c) ——
(d) ——

sepal   petal   stamen   stigma   seed   antenna

(a) *Seed*
(b) *petal*
(c)
(d)

• 6 •

TEST 1   LEVELS 3 to 4

3

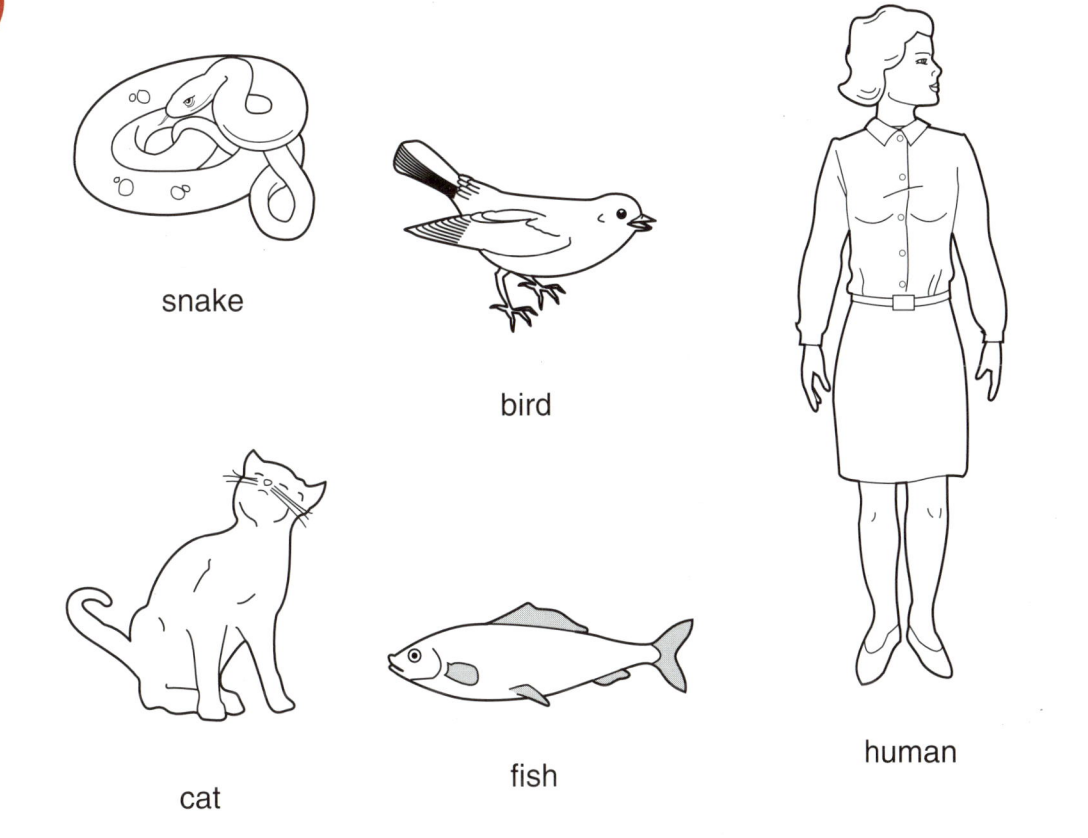

snake

bird

cat

fish

human

What can **all** these animals do?

Tick the **five** correct answers below.

grow   [✓] ✏
run   [ ]
move   [✓]
breathe   [✓]
lay eggs   [ ]
talk   [ ]
produce young [✓]
feed   [✓]

· 7 ·

TEST 1   LEVELS 3 to 4

Materials

4

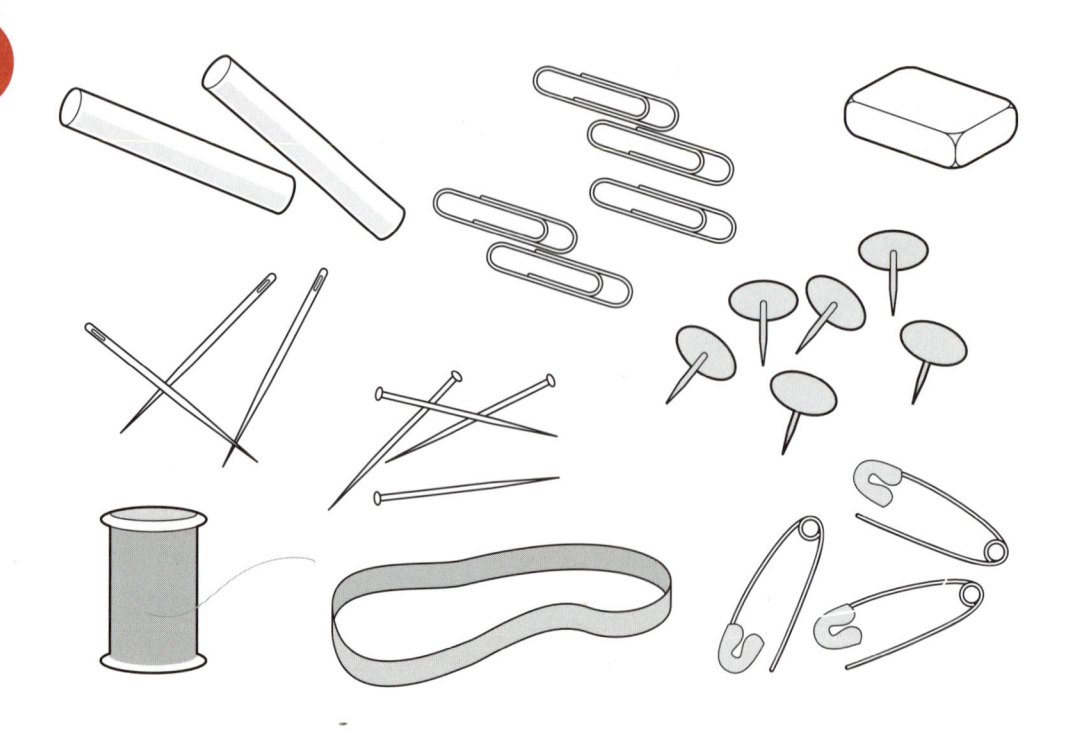

Jo found these objects under the teacher's desk.
She decided to use a magnet to clear up the mess.

Which **five** objects will her magnet pick up? Tick them in the box below.

	could pick up
needles	✓
thread	☐
pins	✓
paper clips	✓
drawing pins	✓
eraser	☐
chalk	☐
elastic band	☐
safety pins	✓

TEST 1 LEVELS 3 to 4

5 Tom put some soil into a jam jar. He added water, shook the jar and left it overnight. The next day he saw that the soil and water had made four separate layers.

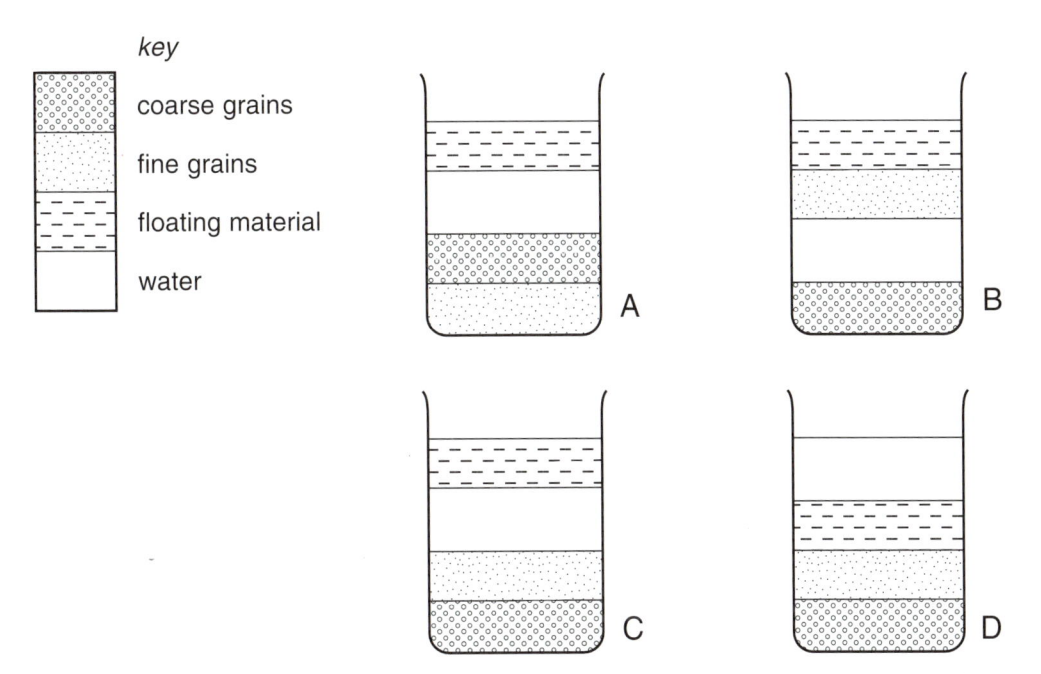

key
- coarse grains
- fine grains
- floating material
- water

A   B   C   D

One of the diagrams shows how the layers settled.

(a) Tick to show the correct answer.

✏️   A   B   C ✓   D

(b) Tom shook the jar again to make the water muddy. How can the soil be separated from the water?

(i) Describe in words.

✏️ _____

_____

(ii) Draw a diagram.

· 9 ·

TEST 1   LEVELS 3 to 4

Sun and light

6

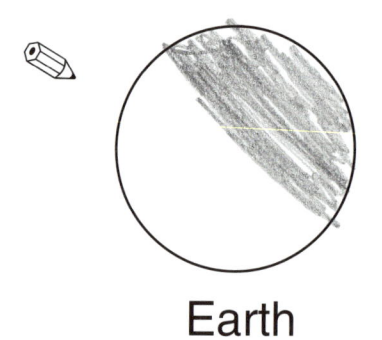

Earth

Sun

(a) Which part of the Earth is in darkness?

Shade the correct part of the drawing above.

(b) Explain what happens as night time changes to day time.

_____
_____
_____
_____
_____

Electricity

7 Only one of these bulbs will light up.

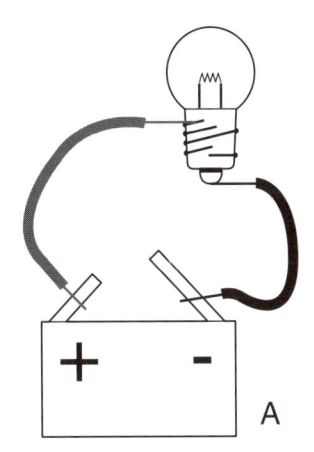

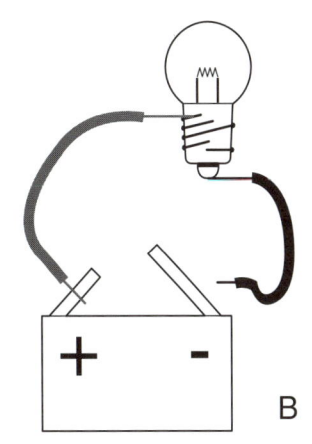

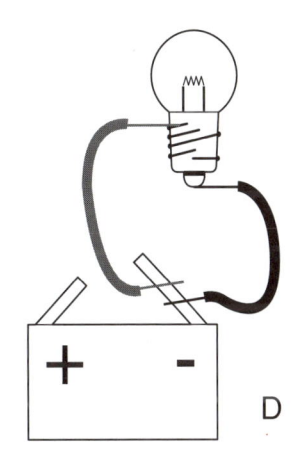

A

B

C

D

(a) Tick the box to show which one will light.

A ☐   B ☐   C ✓   D ☐

(b) Explain your answer.

one wire has to bee conected to the negitive and the other to the plus.

TEST 1 LEVELS 3 to 4

Forces

8

Dina is testing her boat. She blows gently on the sail through a straw.

(a) What happens to her boat?

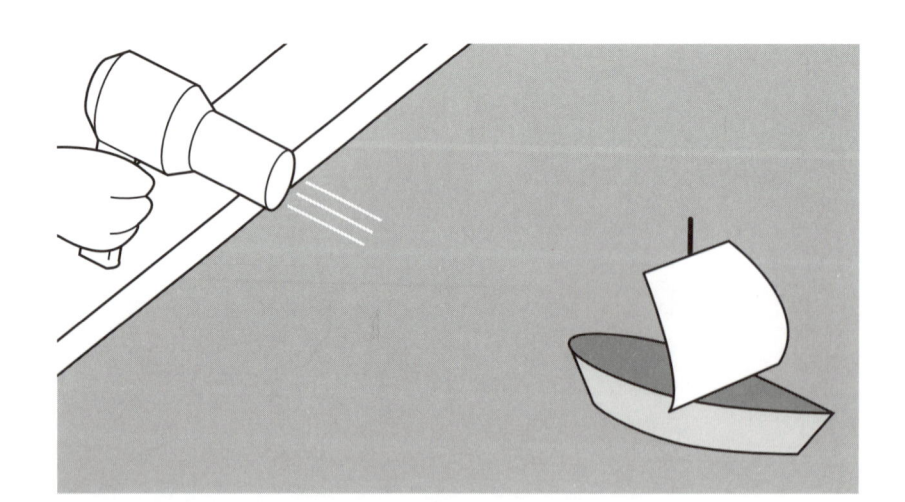

it moves while she is blowing it.

Now she uses a hairdryer.

(b) In what way does the movement of the boat change?

it would go alote faster and further.

TEST 2 LEVELS 3 to 4

Test 2

Time started
Time finished

Living things

1 Look carefully at these diagrams of minibeasts.

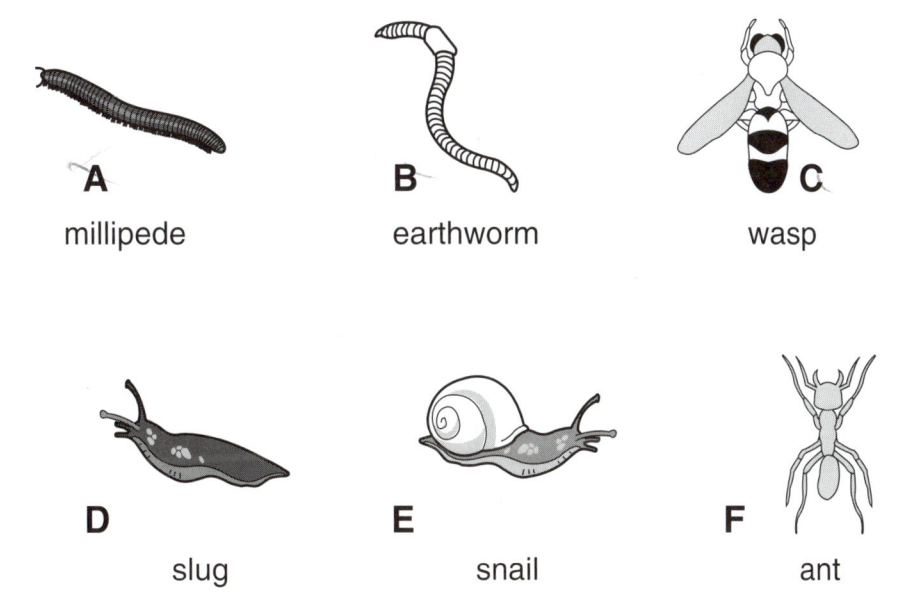

A millipede

B earthworm

C wasp

D slug

E snail

F ant

This key helps you identify different animals.

Write the letter of the correct minibeast in each of the boxes.

Two have been done for you.

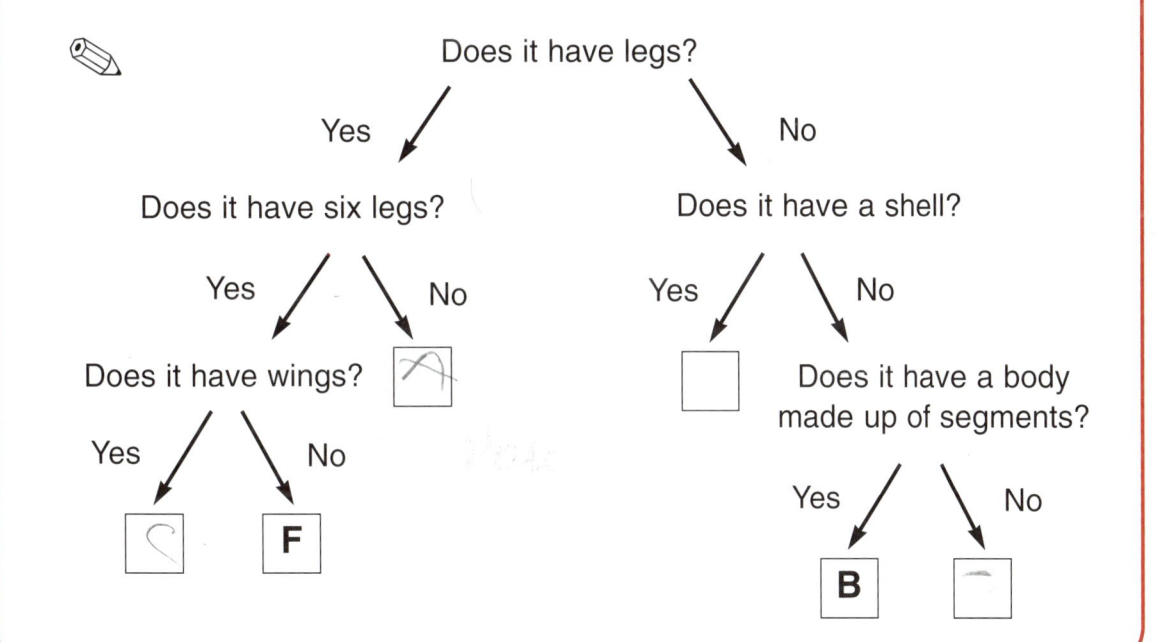

Does it have legs?

Yes → Does it have six legs?

No → Does it have a shell?

Does it have six legs?
Yes → Does it have wings?
No → [A]

Does it have wings?
Yes → [C]
No → [F]

Does it have a shell?
Yes → [ ]
No → Does it have a body made up of segments?

Does it have a body made up of segments?
Yes → [B]
No → [ ]

• 13 •

2 This diagram shows some organs in a human body.

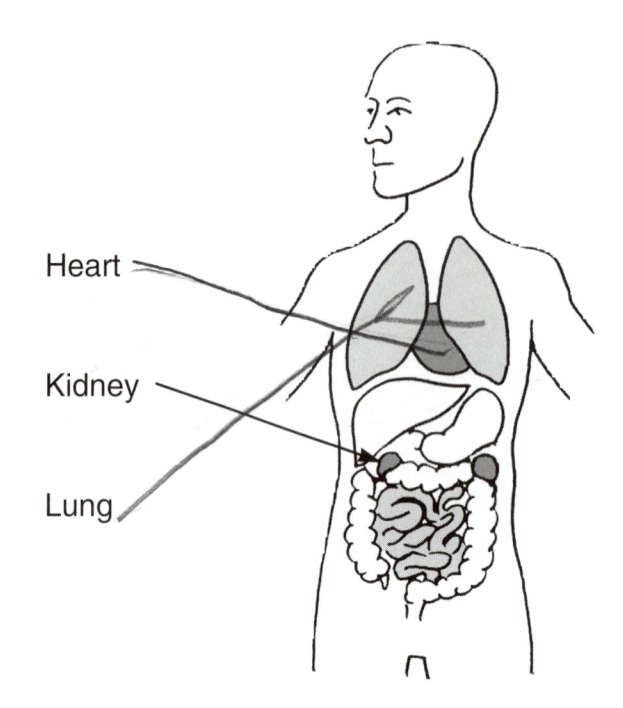

(a) Use an arrow to show the position of:

(i) the heart

(ii) a lung

(b) Write down the main job of the heart.

.... *pump blood around your* ....
.... *body* ....

3 We need food to stay alive.

Write down three more reasons why we need food.

(a) ....

(b) ....

(c) ....

TEST 2   LEVELS 3 to 4

Materials

4 Some things change and can go back to what they were.
Some things change but can never go back to what they were before.

Peas are frozen

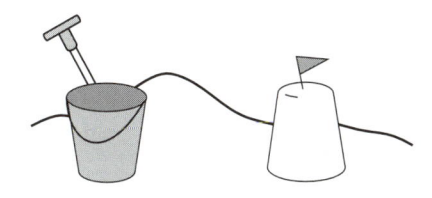

A sand castle is made

An ice cube melts

A cake is baked

An egg fries

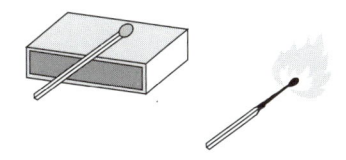

A match is burned

Which of these can change back? Which cannot change back? Tick the box below. One has been done for you.

	can change back	cannot change back
An egg fries		✓
An ice cube melts	✓	
A sand castle is made	✓	
A cake is baked		✓
Peas are frozen	✓	
A match is burned		✓

· 15 ·

TEST 2   LEVELS 3 to 4

Forces

5

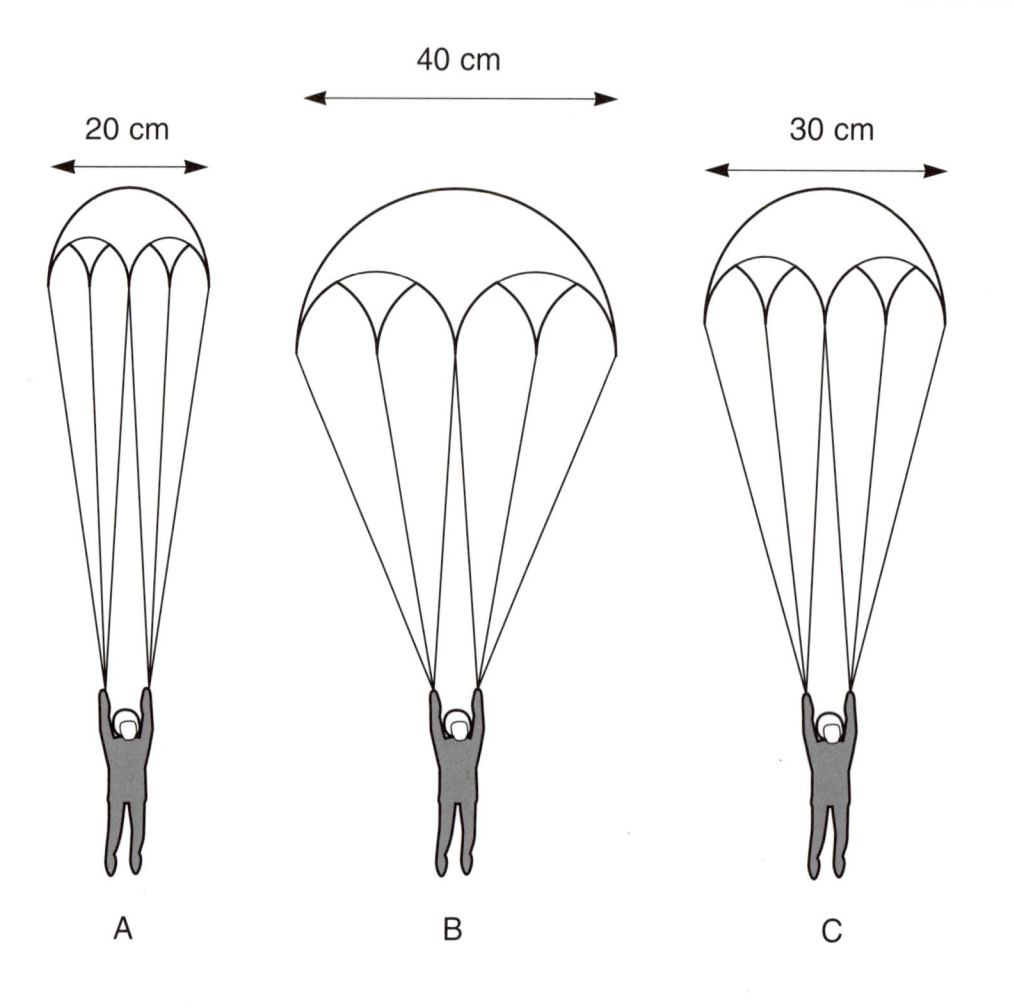

20 cm

40 cm

30 cm

A   B   C

These parachutes were dropped together from the same height.

(a) Which parachute will be last to land?

✎ B

(b) Choose the correct answer to finish this sentence.

This parachute will be the last to land because:

☐ (i) it is the heaviest

✓ (ii) it is the biggest and the air has more effect on it

☐ (iii) it is the lightest

TEST 2 LEVELS 3 to 4

6

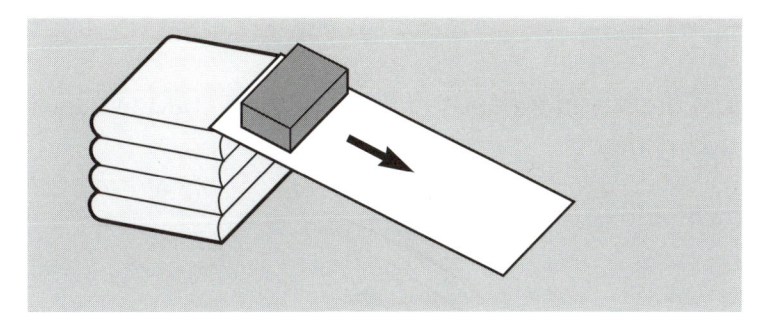

Some children were sliding a wooden block down a ramp.

(a) Name the force which causes the wooden block to move.

✎ _____

Now they put two elastic bands around the block and try again.

They saw that the block moved more slowly.

(b) Name the force which makes it do this.

✎ _____

They covered the block in different materials. They measured how far the block travelled along the table. They recorded their results in a chart.

Material used to cover the block	Distance block travelled along the table
sandpaper	5 cm
plastic	13 cm
shiny paper	12 cm
cotton	8 cm

(c) Name the material which has the greatest resistance to movement.

✎ _____

(d) Name the material which allowed the block to move the fastest.

✎ _____

TEST 2 LEVELS 3 to 4

Sun and light

7 Some children drew and measured the length of shadows at different times on a sunny day.

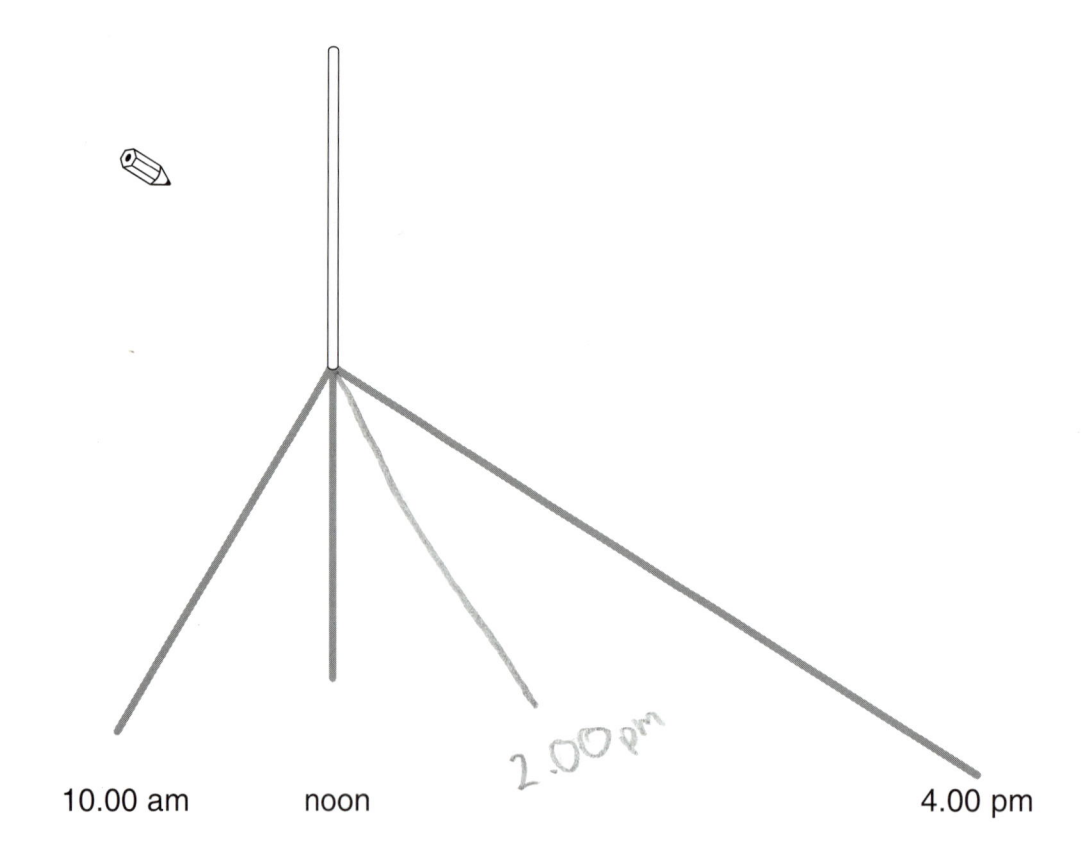

10.00 am   noon   2.00 pm   4.00 pm

(a) Draw the shadow formed at 2.00 pm.

(b) Why is the shadow shorter at noon?

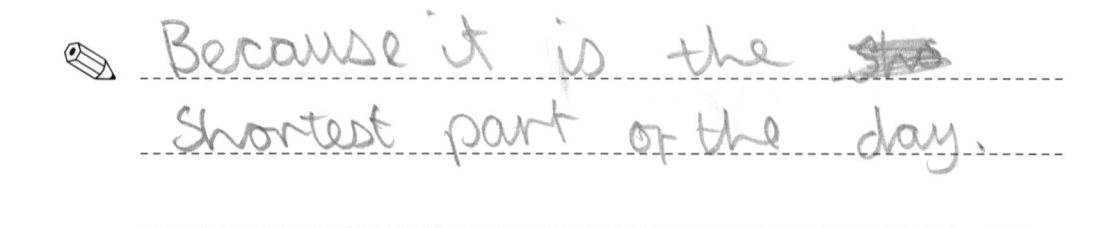

Because it is the shortest part of the day.

TEST 2   LEVELS 3 to 4

Electricity

8

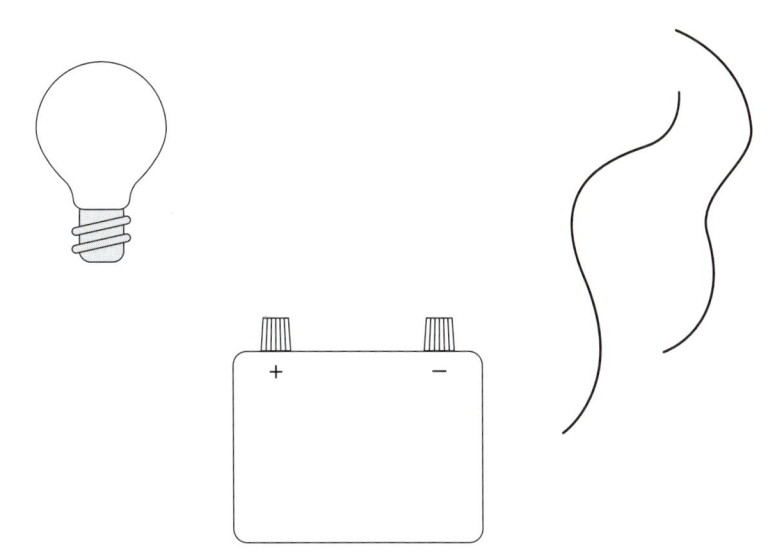

(a) Draw a picture or diagram to show how you would use these to make the light bulb shine.

Now you use two light bulbs.

(b) Will the light from each bulb be:

(i) brighter? ☐

(ii) dimmer? ☐

(iii) the same? ✓

TEST 3   LEVELS 3, 4 and 5

• Test 3 •

Time started
Time finished

Living things

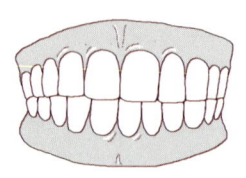

1

We use our front teeth to bite off chunks of food.

(a) What do we use our back teeth for?

✏ _grind_

Plaque forms on our teeth. It is caused by food, bacteria and acid.

(b) How can we get rid of plaque?

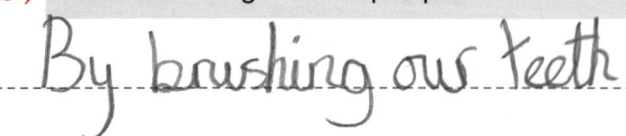

By brushing our teeth

(c) What might happen if we don't remove plaque?

(i) _You teeth might fall out_

(ii) _They go black_

2

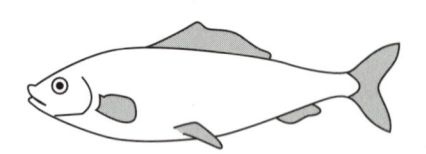

Fish live in water. They have gills so they can breathe.

Explain two other ways fish are suited to life in water.

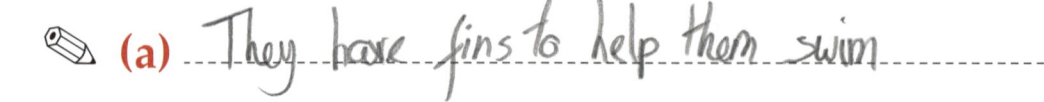

✏ **(a)** _They have fins to help them swim_

(b) _There Their scales are waterproof_

• 20 •

3 These plants look very different.

bluebell

oak tree

moss

seaweed

grass

fern

rose

Tick **three** boxes to show ways in which they are the same.

they can take in nutrients	✓
they have stem and leaves	
they have flowers	
they grow	✓
they reproduce	✓
they lose their leaves in winter	

Materials

4

Some children tested different powders to see if they would dissolve in water. The chart below shows their results.

Powder	after shaking in cold water	after heating liquid
white sugar	slightly cloudy	clear, colourless
flour	lumpy, cloudy	lumpy, white
instant coffee	dark brown, some solid lumps	clear brown
salt	slightly cloudy	clear, colourless
ground pepper	slightly coloured, bits floating	slightly coloured, bits floating and sinking

Look carefully at their results.

Name two powders which do not form a solution in water.

(a) _____

(b) _____

TEST 3 LEVELS 3, 4 and 5

Electricity

5 Some materials allow electricity to pass through them easily. We say these materials are good electrical conductors.

(a) Tick the correct boxes to complete this chart.

Object	will conduct electricity
plastic	
aluminium foil	
paperclip	
wooden ruler	
key	
nail	
paper	

(b) How can you use the results to help sort these objects into metals or non-metals?

✎ ....

6

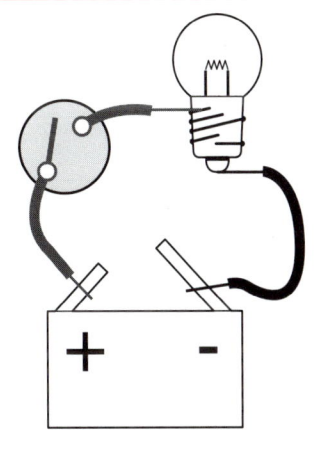

Write down two things that will happen when the switch is turned on.

✎ (a) The light will turn on

(b) The circit will be complete

TEST 3 LEVELS 3, 4 and 5

Sound

7 Gita can hear trains going past her bedroom window, even though the window is shut.

(a) Choose the best answer to finish this sentence.

Sound reached her ears by travelling through:

(i) ☐ air

(ii) ☐ glass

(iii) ☑ air and glass

(iv) ☐ the bedroom door

Gita moved to the spare bed.

(b) Why do the trains seem quieter now?

Because Gita is further away from the trains now.

TEST 3   LEVELS 3, 4 and 5

Sun and light

8 Anoush and Jackson shone light at some models they made. They switched the torch on.

(a) Draw what they saw on the screen.

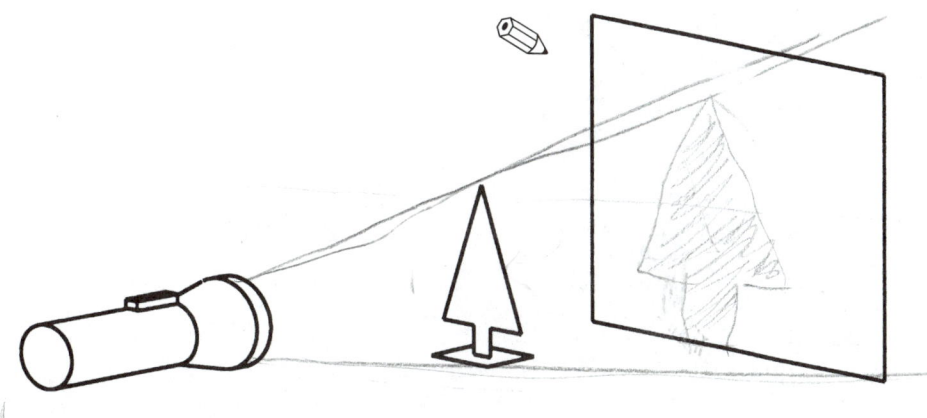

(b) Why did this happen?

Because the torch is on an angle

They moved the tree nearer to the screen.

(c) What change do they see now?

The shadow will be bigger.

They made a flower from clear plastic. They switched the torch on.

(d) Can they see the torch through the flower?

(e) Tick the box to finish this sentence correctly.

The tree is made from:

(i) a transparent material ✓

(ii) an opaque material

(iii) a translucent material ✓

· 25 ·

TEST 4 LEVELS 3, 4 and 5

Test 4

Time started
Time finished

Living things

1

Look carefully at the picture. The diagram shows three stages in the life cycle of a duck.

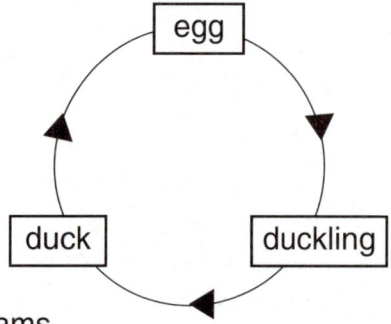

Now finish these diagrams.

(a) The life cycle of humans.

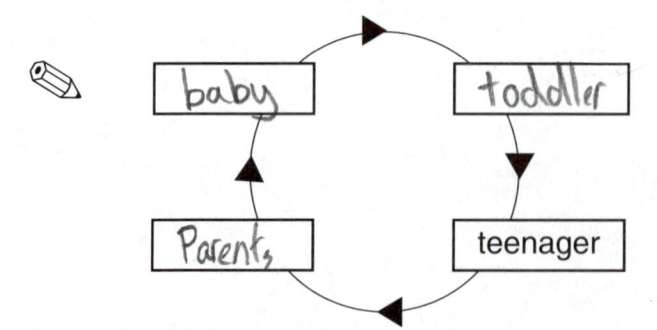

[handwritten: baby, toddler, Parents, teenager]

(b) The life cycle of a frog.

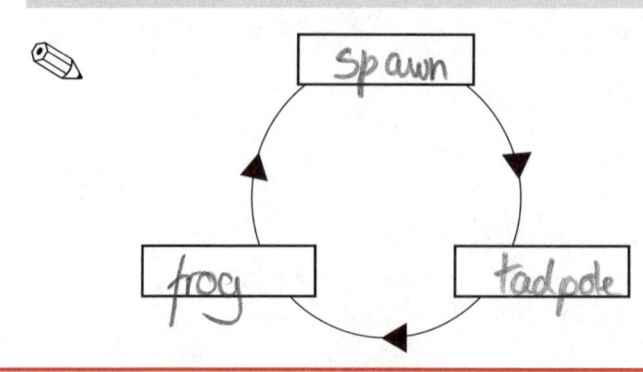

[handwritten: spawn, frog, tadpole]

• 26 •

TEST 4 LEVELS 3, 4 and 5

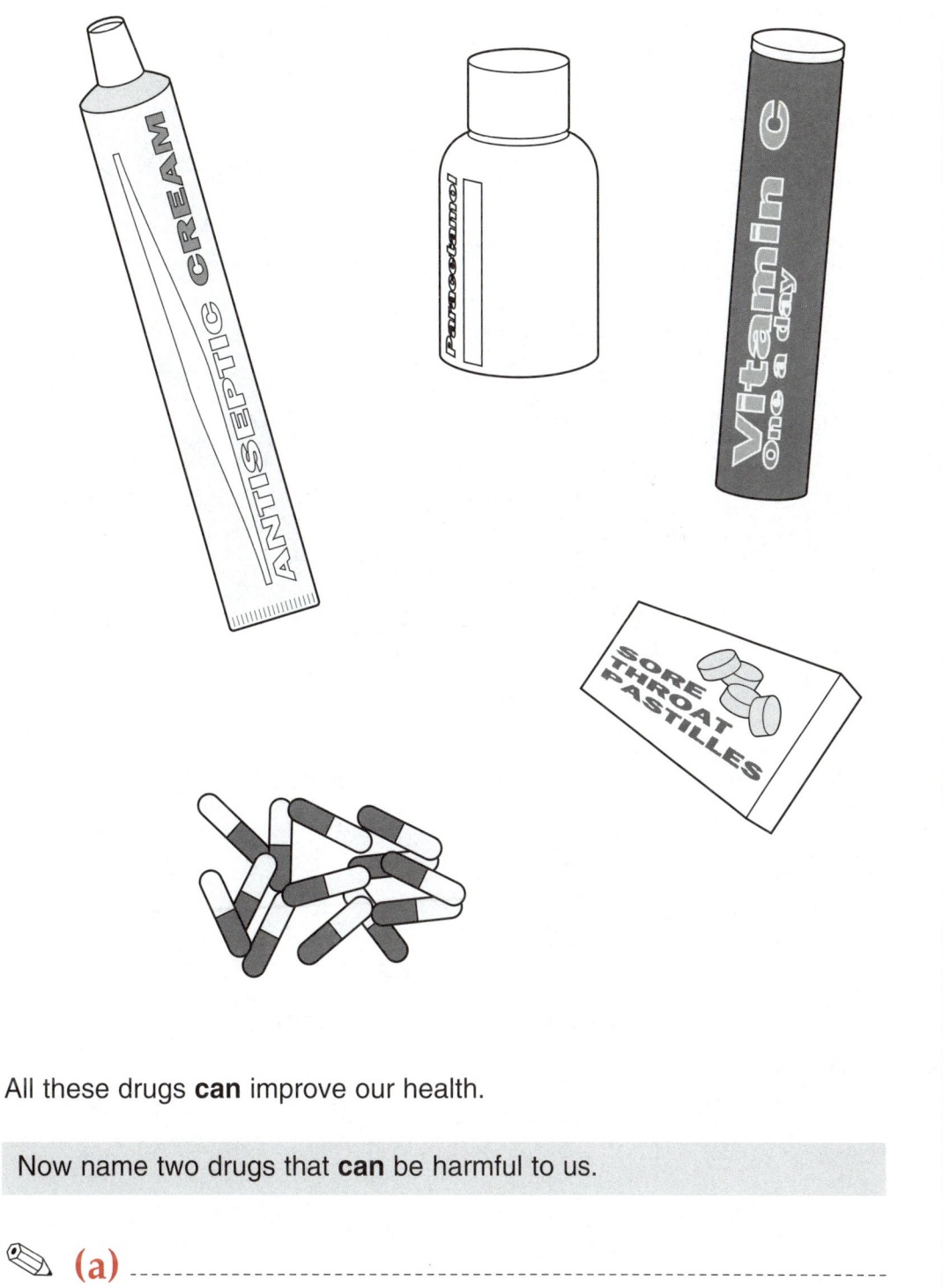

2

All these drugs **can** improve our health.

Now name two drugs that **can** be harmful to us.

✎ **(a)** ....

✎ **(b)** ....

3

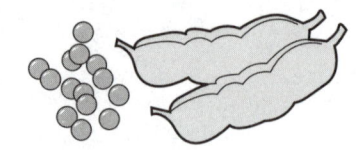

After a short time the fresh peas will rot.

(a) What causes this to happen?

(b) Explain how freezing helps preserve them.

(c) Explain how drying peas preserves them.

(d) Give **two** reasons why tinned peas don't rot.

(i)

(ii)

TEST 4   LEVELS 3, 4 and 5

Materials

4 Cars are made from different materials.

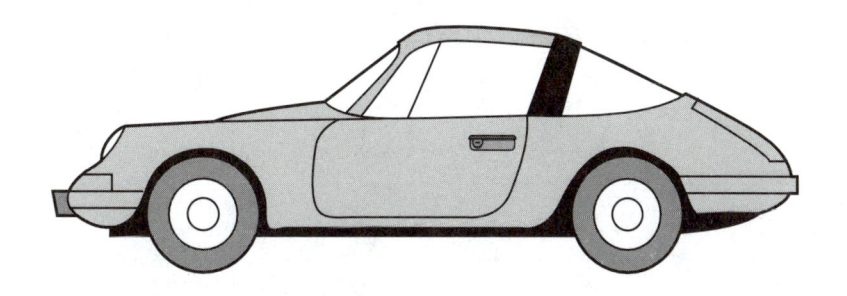

Tick one box to complete each sentence.

(a) Glass is used for windows because:

- it keeps the rain out ☐
- it is transparent (see through) ☐
- it is warm ☐
- it is strong ☐

(b) Rubber is used for tyres because:

- it grips well ☐
- it is waterproof ☐
- it does not wear out ☐
- it is strong ☐

(c) Steel is used for the body because:

- it is shiny ☐
- it can be painted different colours ☐
- it breaks easily ☐
- it is strong ☐

5 The chart shows different properties of three substances.

	flows easily through tube	has its own shape	can be squashed into a smaller space
Substance A	✗	✓	✗
Substance B	✓	✗	✓
Substance C	✓	✗	✗

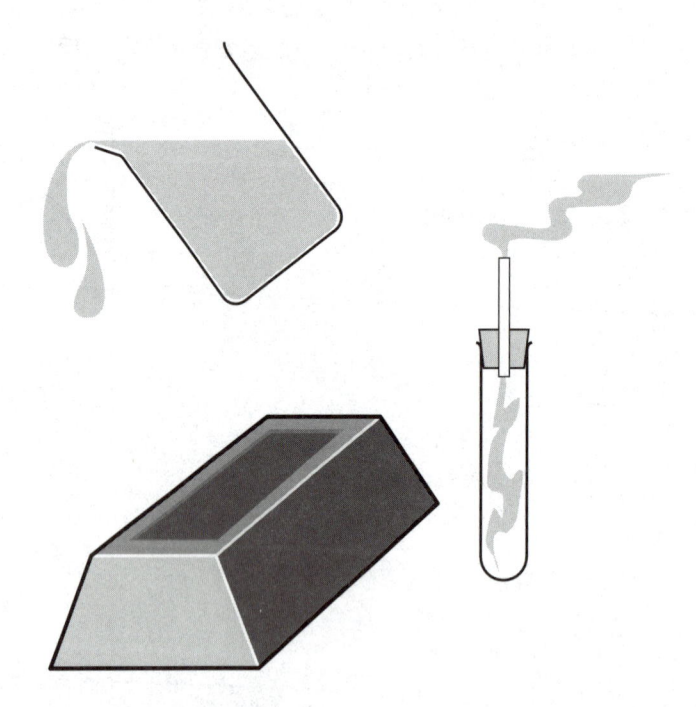

Tick a box to show whether each substance is a solid, a liquid or a gas.

	solid	liquid	gas
Substance A			
Substance B			
Substance C			

Sound

6

dried peas

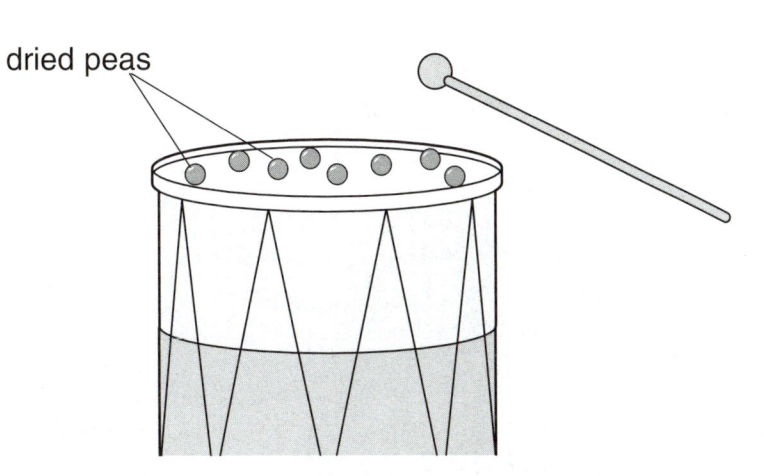

(a) What happens to the dried peas when the drum is banged?

The drum is banged again, even harder.

(b) What do the peas do this time?

(c) What is different about the sound the drum makes this time?

TEST 4   LEVELS 3, 4 and 5

Forces

7

(a) What does Matthew do to Jack to get him back in the box?

✏️ ....

(b) What happens to the spring?

✏️ ....

Matthew undoes the hook. Two things happen:
• the lid opens
• Jack 'leaps' out of the box.

(c) Explain why this happens.

✏️ ....

....

....

· 32 ·

TEST 5 LEVELS 4 and 5

Test 5

Time started
Time finished

Living things

1 Jennifer put cress seeds onto three damp cotton wool pads.

She put each one in a cardboard box.

Box A has a slit in the top.

Box B has a slit in the side.

Box C has no slits.

After five days she looked at her cress seeds.

✏ ------------   ------------   ------------

Write A, B or C under each picture to show which box the seeds had been put in.

2 Kit measured his pulse rate after different activities.

Join the activity to the correct pulse rate.

One has been done for you.

Activity (5 minutes)	**Pulse rate** (beats per minute)
jogging	89
walking	79
lying down	126
sitting writing	108

· 33 ·

3 All these animals have a skeleton.

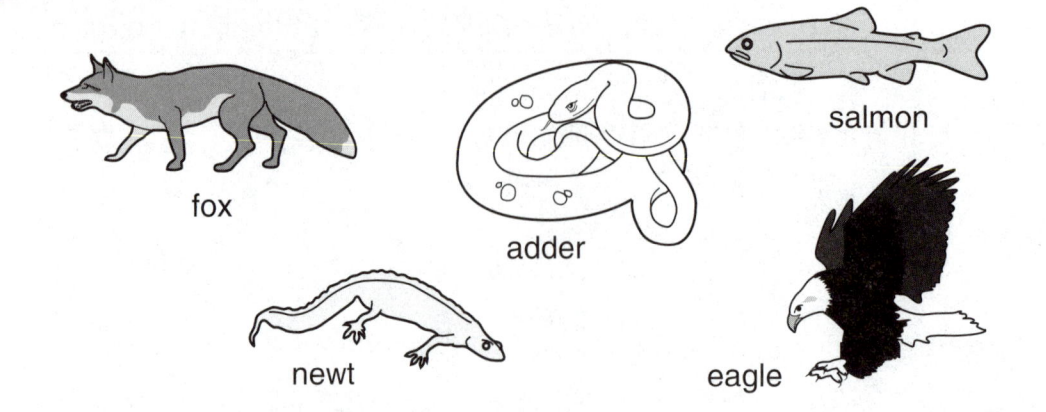

fox
adder
salmon
newt
eagle

Use the key below to answer these questions.

Which animal:

(a) is warm-blooded and doesn't have feathers?

✎ _____

(b) has scaly skin and uses gills for breathing?

✎ _____

(c) doesn't have scaly skin or feathers *and* is cold blooded?

✎ _____

A key to identify animals.

Is the animal warm blooded?

Yes → / No →

Does it have feathers?   Does it have scaly skin?

Yes / No   Yes / No

BIRDS   MAMMALS   Does it have gills for breathing?   AMPHIBIANS
(eagle)   (fox)   (newt)

Yes / No

FISH   REPTILES
(salmon)   (adder)

TEST 5 LEVELS 4 and 5

Materials

4 The Patels have moved into a new house. They want to plant a garden. The builders have left a lot of stones and gravel in the soil.

(a) How can they separate the gravel and stones from the soil?

✎ ....

(b) They want to separate the gravel from the larger stones. Describe a way they can do this.

✎ ....
....
....
....

5

garden wire

electrical wire

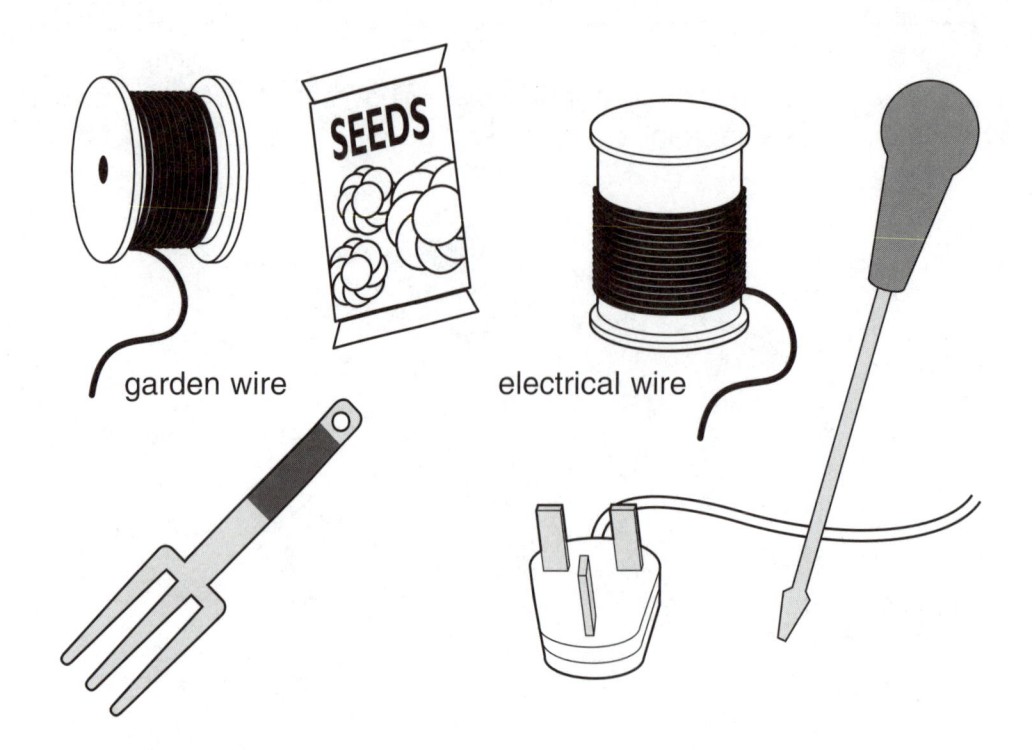

Both wires in the picture above have been coated in plastic.

Why do they have this plastic coating?

Give a **different** reason for each.

(a) the garden wire

✎ ....
....
....

(b) the electrical wire

✎ ....
....
....
....

6

Sarah added salt to water until no more would dissolve.

How can she:

(a) get the salt back?

....

....

....

(b) get pure water back?

....

....

....

....

Forces

7

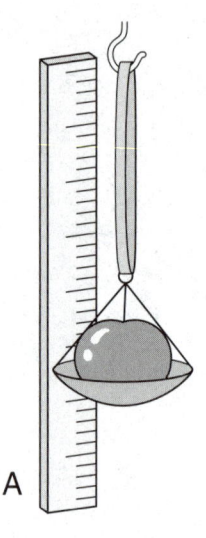

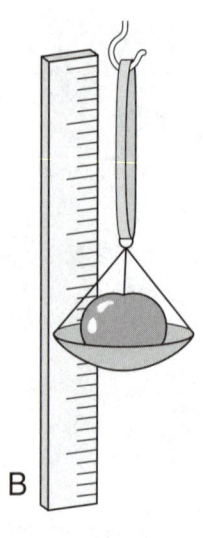

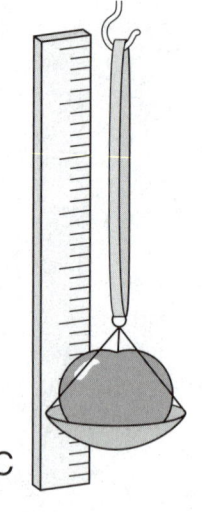

Some children were comparing the weight of tomatoes they had grown.

(a) Name the force that is giving the tomatoes their weight.

....

....

(b) Why is C the heaviest?

....

....

(c) Draw two arrows to show two forces acting on the tomato.

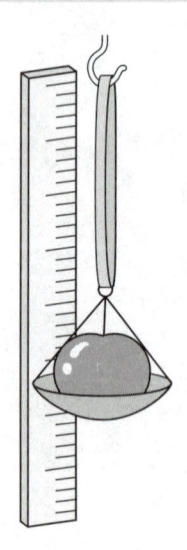

TEST 5   LEVELS 4 and 5

Sound

8

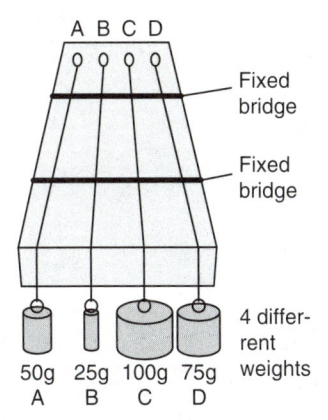

[Diagram: musical instrument with 4 strings A, B, C, D over two fixed bridges, with 4 different weights hanging: 50g A, 25g B, 100g C, 75g D]

The four strings used on this musical instrument are exactly the same. We hear a sound when each string is plucked.

(a) How do we hear the sound?

....

....

....

(b) Which string gives the highest pitch?

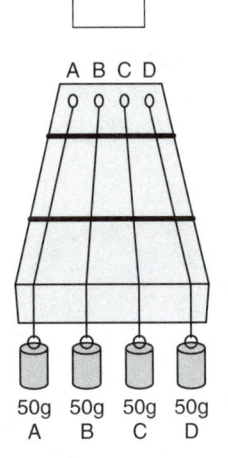

☐

[Diagram: same instrument with 4 strings A, B, C, D and equal weights: 50g A, 50g B, 50g C, 50g D]

Now all the weights are the same.

(c) How can you produce notes of a different pitch?

....

....

....

Forces

9 Alice is experimenting with her new train set. The engine and carriages have magnets inside them.

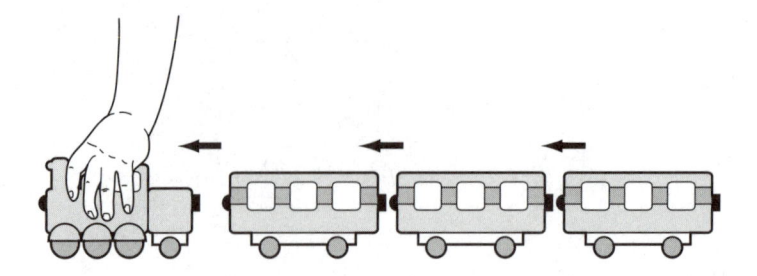

When she arranges them like this, the engine and carriages move towards each other.

(a) Name the force that causes the train to join together.

....

She tries the engine a different way.

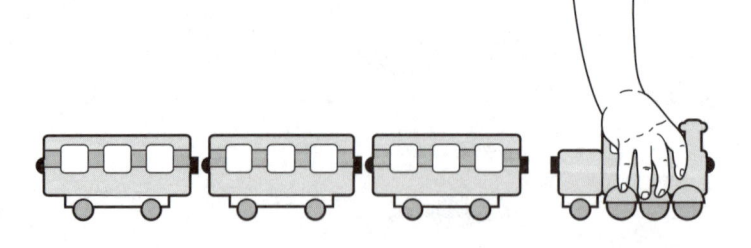

(b) What happens to the carriages as she moves the engine towards them now?

....

....

(c) Explain why this happens.

....

....

....

Test 6

Living things

1

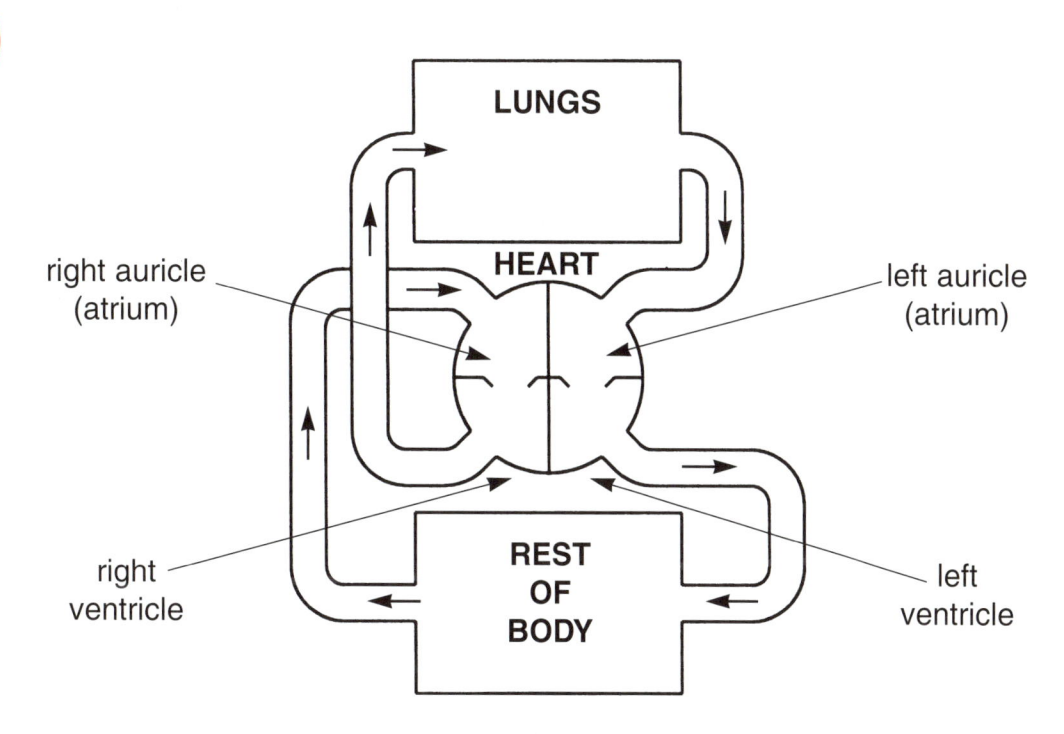

A diagram of the circulatory system

Blood travels round the body in **two** main types of blood vessels: arteries and veins.

(a) Describe the job each type does.

(i) arteries _____

(ii) veins _____

(b) What happens to the blood when it reaches the lungs?

_____

2 Humans have skeletons.

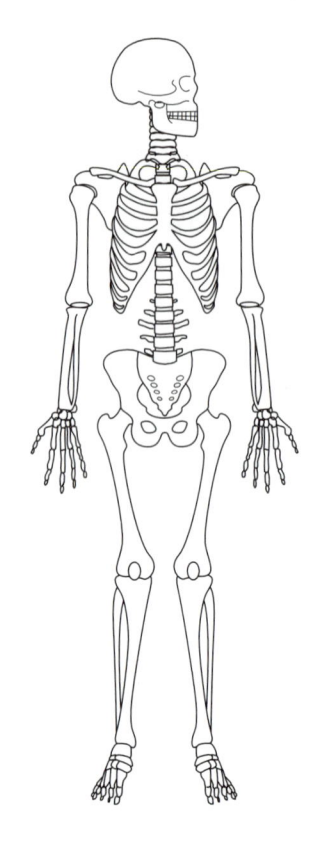

Skeletons are important because:

- they protect parts of the body

- they support parts of the body and keep us upright

- they allow us to move

(a) Name the bones which protect

(i) the brain _____

(ii) the lungs _____

(b) What does the skeleton have which makes us able to move?

_____

(c) What is fixed to the bones to cause movement?

_____

3

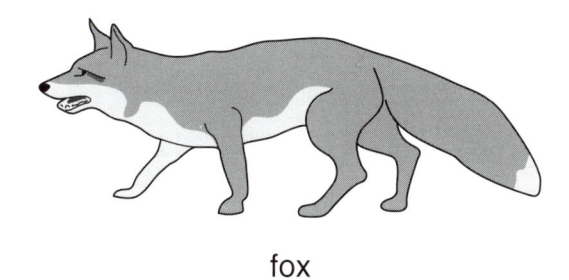

fox

snail

starling

weed

(a) Write these in a food chain.

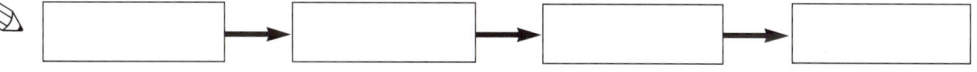

☐ → ☐ → ☐ → ☐

(b) Write the name of:

(i) the producer _____

(ii) a consumer _____

(c) If the farmer sprayed his field with weedkiller, what might happen to the starlings?

_____

_____

TEST 6 LEVELS 4 and 5

Materials

4 Some children were going on a class outing. They wanted to keep their drink warm for a one-hour coach journey.
They carried out an experiment to help them decide how to do this.

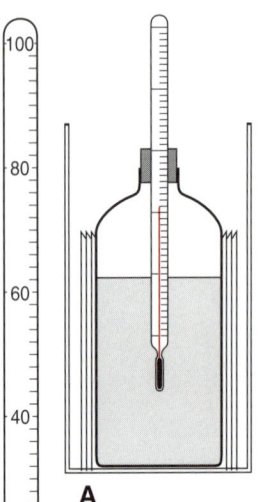

A Bottle wrapped in newspaper
B Bottle wrapped in aluminium foil
C Bottle wrapped in cotton towel
D Bottle wrapped in foam rubber

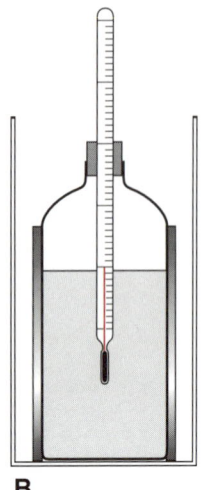

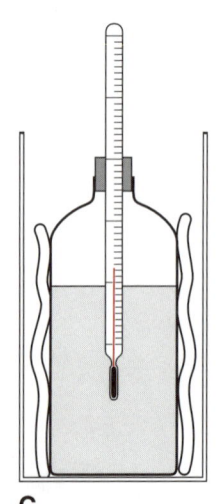

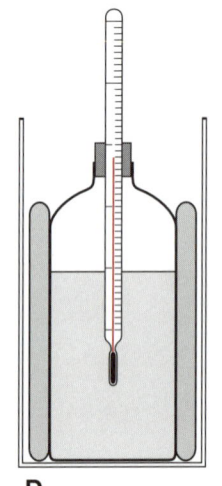

They filled each bottle with water at 65°C. They read the temperature of each bottle after one hour.

(a) Use the big thermometer to read the small thermometers in each of the four bottles.

Write down the results on the chart below.

	starting temperature	temperature after one hour
Bottle A	65°C	
Bottle B	65°C	
Bottle C	65°C	
Bottle D	65°C	

(b) Which material do you think they chose to wrap their drinks?

....

(c) Why did they choose it?

....

....

· 44 ·

Electricity

5

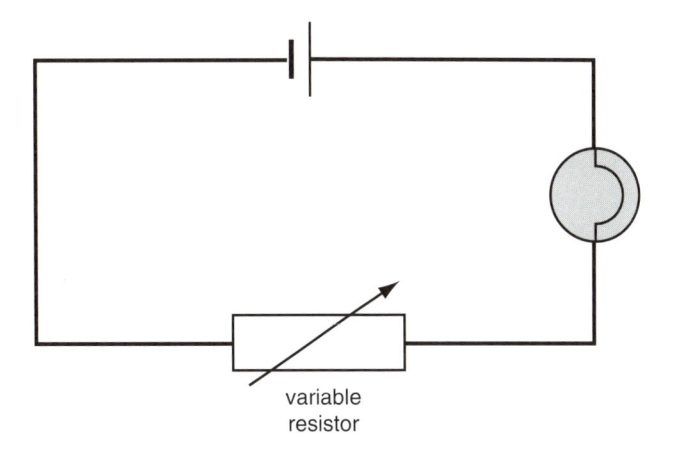

(a) If the variable resistor is increased, does the bulb:

- [ ] (i) become brighter?
- [ ] (ii) not change?
- [ ] (iii) become dimmer?

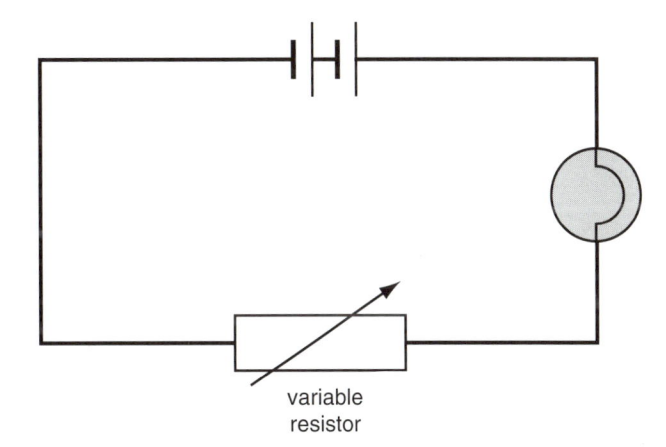

(b) A second battery is included in the circuit. The resistor stays the same.

Does the bulb:

- [ ] (i) become brighter?
- [ ] (ii) not change?
- [ ] (iii) become dimmer?

TEST 6 LEVELS 4 and 5

Sun and light

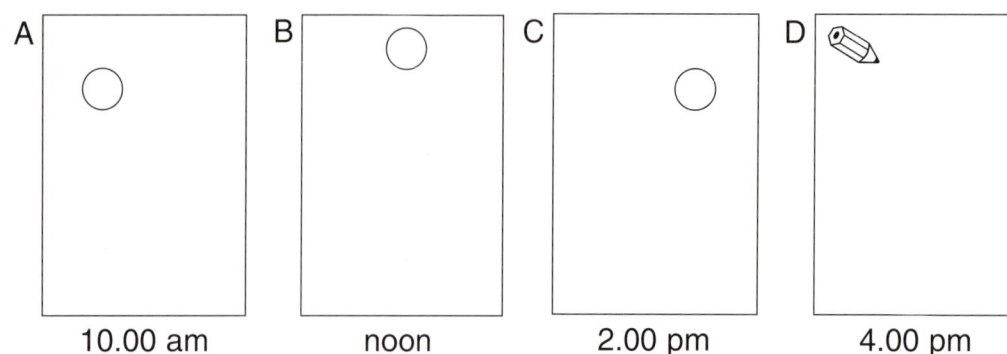

6 In class 6D, some children were plotting the position of the sun through their classroom window.

A	B	C	D
10.00 am	noon	2.00 pm	4.00 pm

They drew three pictures to show where the sun was at 10.00 am, noon and 2.00 pm.

(a) Now draw where the sun will be on the fourth picture.

(b) Explain why the sun appears to move across the sky.

....

....

....

7 Charlotte is drawing a picture.

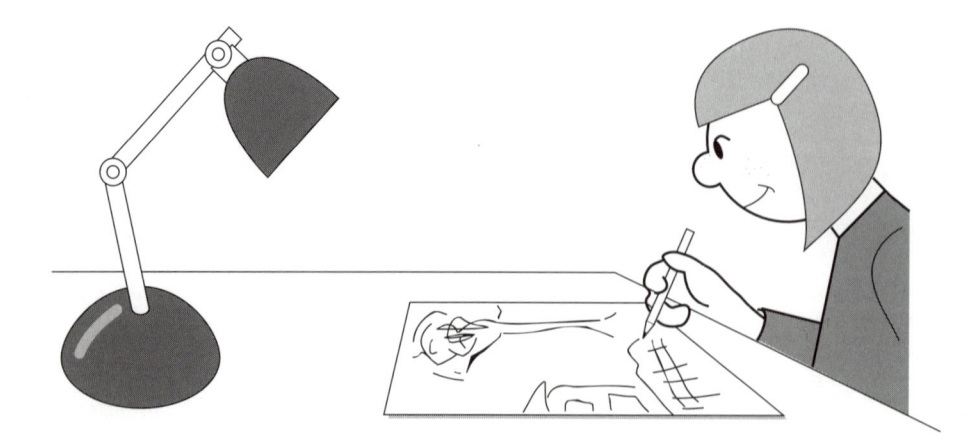

Use arrows to show how Charlotte sees her picture.

Forces

8 Maddy is floating in the water.

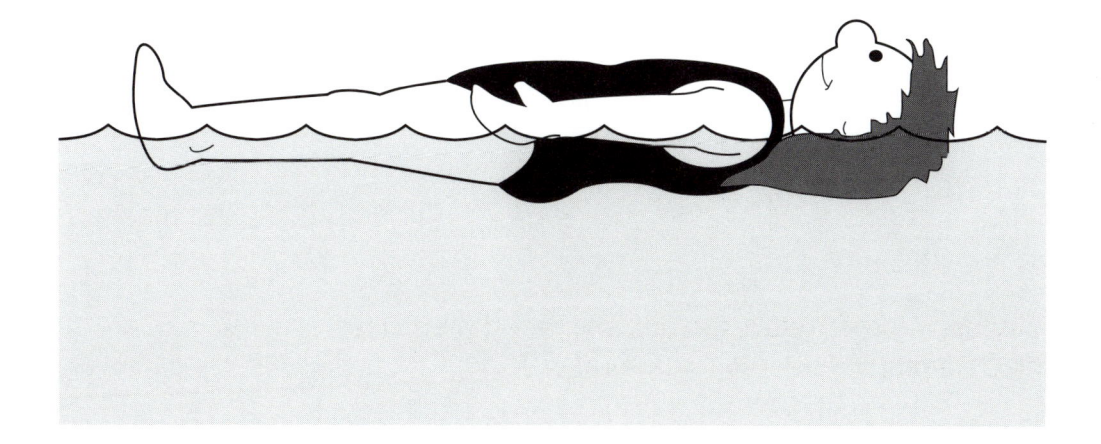

(a) Draw **two** arrows on the drawing above to show the **two** forces on her body.

(b) Why doesn't she sink?

_____

_____

_____

TEST 7   LEVELS 5 and 6

Test 7

Time started
Time finished

Living things

1

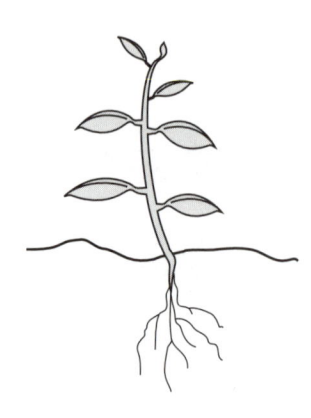

This drawing shows the main parts of a plant.

Describe two functions of the root.

(a) ....

....

(b) ....

....

2 This diagram shows the structure of an animal cell.

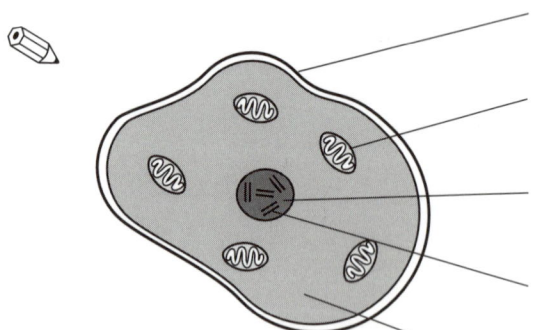

A
B
C
D
E

Choose **five** of the words below to label the diagram correctly.

nucleus   cell wall   cell membrane   chloroplast
mitochondrion   chromosomes   cytoplasm

· 48 ·

3 Class 4D were finding out what lived under stones. They discovered woodlice, slugs and earthworms.

Write three reasons why these creatures choose to live under stones.

(a) ....

(b) ....

(c) ....

4 Hannah and Gwen did an experiment to find out how to stop food going mouldy. They used five slices of bread from a fresh sandwich loaf.
The chart below shows what they did with each slice.

	Conditions for experiment	Number of days for mould to appear
Slice 1	sealed in plastic bag, put in dark cupboard	5
Slice 2	left on table for 2 hrs, sealed in plastic bag, placed in dark cupboard	3
Slice 3	dried in oven, sealed in plastic bag, placed in dark cupboard	no mould within 28 days
Slice 4	sealed in plastic bag, placed in freezer	no mould within 28 days
Slice 5	sealed in plastic bag, placed in fridge.	10

They examined each slice of bread every day and wrote down when mould appeared.
Look carefully at their results in the chart and answer these questions.

(a) What two ways did Hannah and Gwen find to stop the bread going mouldy?

(i) _____

(ii) _____

(b) Why is it important to keep food covered?

_____

_____

_____

_____

Materials

5 Look carefully at the different places we see water in the kitchen.

(a) Now write three states of water shown in the picture.

(i) _____

(ii) _____

(iii) _____

(b) Explain why drops of water are forming on the inside of the window.

_____
_____
_____
_____

6 Sonar devices send out sound waves. They are used for finding things in the ocean.

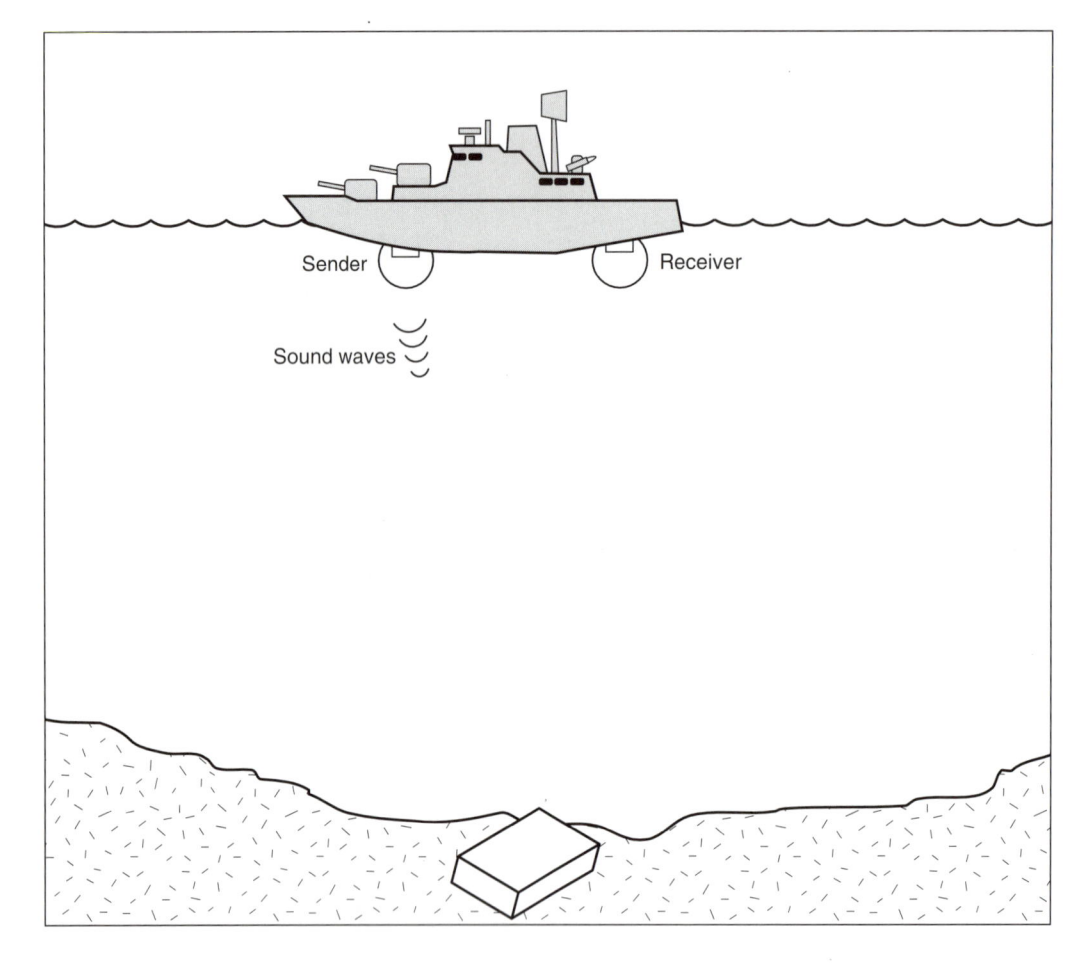

(a) Write down **two** reasons why they can do this.

(i) _____

_____

_____

(ii) _____

_____

_____

(b) Draw arrows on the picture to show what happens.

Electricity

7

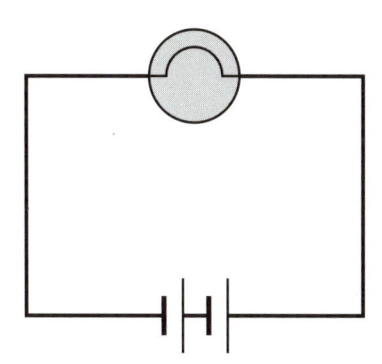

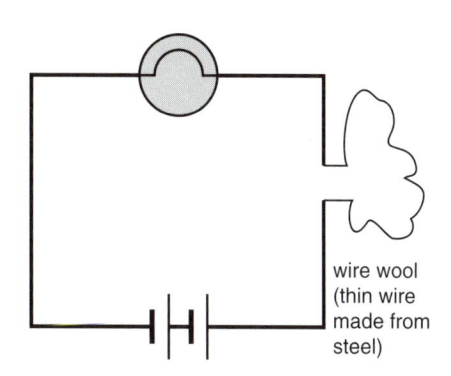

Arran found that when he included a length of wire wool in his circuit, two things happened:

- the bulb became dimmer.
- the wire wool became warmer.

(a) Explain why this happened.

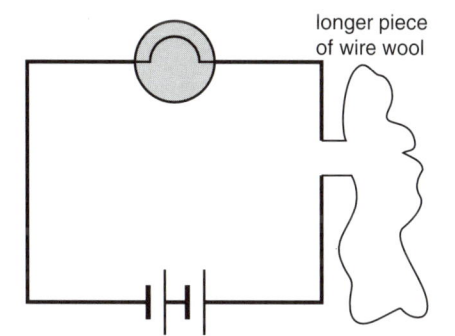

Rosa used a much longer piece of wire wool.

(b) How did her bulb compare with Arran's?

TEST 7 LEVELS 5 and 6

Sun and light

8

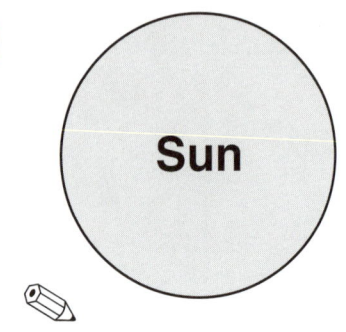

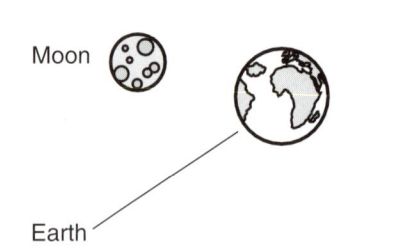

(a) (i) Draw a line and arrows on the diagram above to show the movement of the Moon during one month.

(ii) How long does it take for the Moon to reach **position X** on the diagram above?

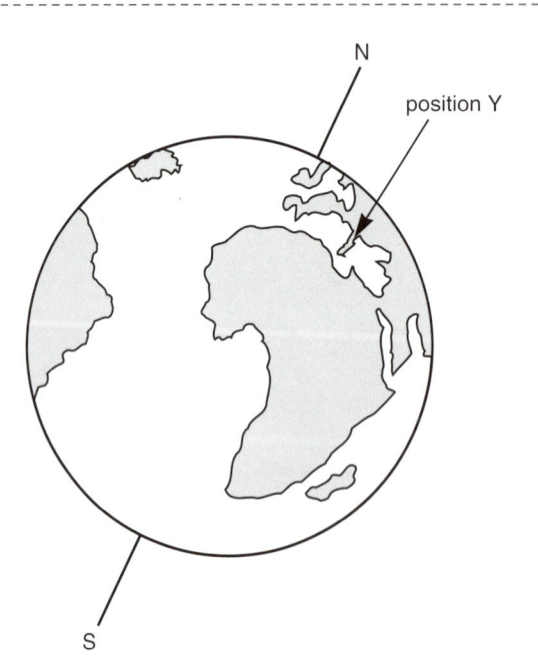

The Earth is tilted on its axis as it orbits the Sun.

(b) If you lived at **position Y** on the Earth (see diagram), what change would you see in the course of a year as a result of the Earth's tilted axis?

TEST 1   Level 3 and 4

• Answers to Test 1 •

1 Living things
(a) lettuce → snail → thrush
(b) thrush

2 Living things
(a) stamen
(b) petal
(c) stigma
(d) sepal

3 Living things
grow, move, breathe, produce young, feed
(5 marks)

4 Materials
needles, pins, paper clips, drawing pins, safety pins
(5 marks)

5 Materials
(a) C
(b) (i) filter the muddy water/evaporate the water
   (ii)

   fine cloth or filter paper + funnel — soil, water   or   saucer left in warm place or heated

6 The sun and light
(a)

   Sun   Earth

(b) The Earth spins around (on its axis) so the part that was facing from the Sun turns towards the Sun, and the Sun's light is shining on it.

7 Electricity
(a) A
(b) A is the only one to have a complete circuit.

8 Forces
(a) The boat moves away from her.
(b) The boat moves further away from her/more quickly / The boat speeds up.

TEST 1

	8-12 questions correct	working towards Level 3
16 x Level 3	13-16 questions correct	satisfactory Level 3
9 x Level 4	16-25 questions correct	good Level 3

• 55 •

TEST 2   Level 3 and 4

Answers to Test 2

1 Living things

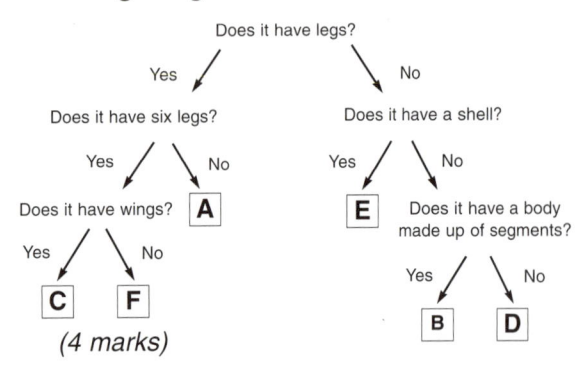

Does it have legs?
- Yes → Does it have six legs?
  - Yes → Does it have wings?
    - Yes → **C**
    - No → **F**
  - No → **A**
- No → Does it have a shell?
  - Yes → **E**
  - No → Does it have a body made up of segments?
    - Yes → **B**
    - No → **D**

(4 marks)

2 Living things
(a) heart, kidney, lung labelled on body diagram

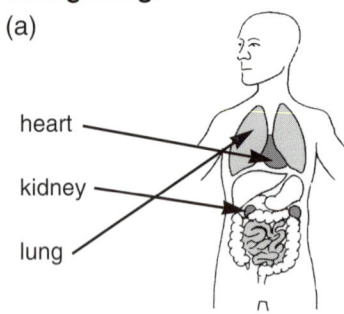

(2 marks)

(b) It pumps blood around the body.

3 Living things
(a) to give us energy
(b) to grow
(c) to keep us healthy

4 Materials

	can change back	cannot change back
An egg fries		✓
An ice cube melts	✓	
A sand castle is made	✓	
A cake is baked		✓
Peas are frozen	✓	
A match is burned		✓

(5 marks)

5 Forces
(a) B
(b) (ii) It is the biggest and the air has more effect on it.

6 Forces
(a) gravity/gravitational force
(b) friction
(c) sandpaper
(d) plastic

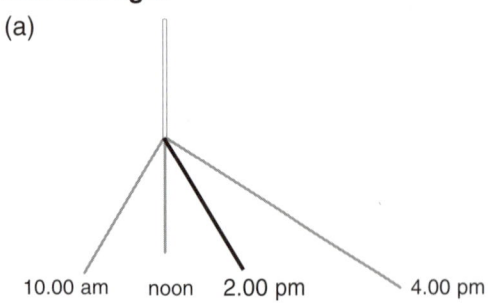

7 Sun and light
(a) shadow diagram at 10.00 am, noon, 2.00 pm, 4.00 pm
(b) The sun is higher in the sky at noon and so causes the shadow to be shorter.

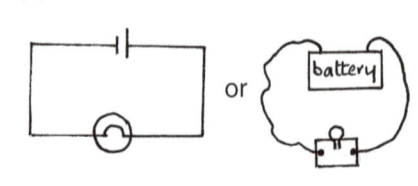

8 Electricity
(a) circuit diagram or battery drawing
(b) (ii) – dimmer.

TEST 2

	7-10 questions correct	working towards Level 3
14 x Level 3	11-13 questions correct	satisfactory Level 3
11 x Level 4	14-25 questions correct	good Level 3

• 56 •

Answers to Test 3

1. **Living things**
   (a) to grind tough food / to make food soft
   (b) by brushing our teeth and/or using an anti-plaque mouthwash
   (c) (i) Our teeth will decay. (ii) Holes/cavities/bad breath/gum disease will form.
   (Accept any two answers in (i) and (ii).)

2. **Living things**
   (a) They have fins so they can swim / to help them swim.
   (b) Their bodies are streamlined.

3. **Living things**
   – they can take in nutrients
   – they grow
   – they reproduce
   (3 marks)

4. **Materials**
   (a) flour
   (b) ground pepper

5. **Materials**
   (a) aluminium foil, paper clip, key, nail
   (4 marks)
   (b) metals conduct electricity

6. **Electricity**
   (a) Electricity/current flows around the circuit.
   (b) The light comes on.

7. **Sound**
   (a) (iii) air and glass
   (b) because the spare bed is further away from the window/train. Sounds get fainter/quieter the further they are away from the source.

8. **Sun and light**
   (a) 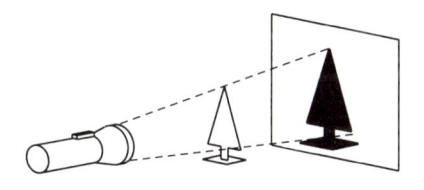
   (b) Light can't pass through the (cardboard) model and so a shadow is formed.
   (c) The shadow is smaller.
   (d) Yes
   (e) (ii) an opaque material

TEST 3

6 × Level 3	6-9 questions correct	working towards Level 4
10 × Level 4	10-16 questions correct	satisfactory Level 4
9 × Level 5	17-25 questions correct	good Level 4, some Level 5

Answers to Test 4

1 Living things

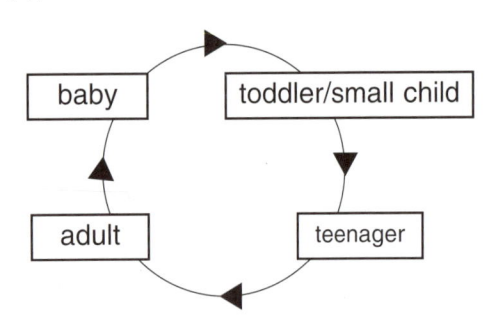

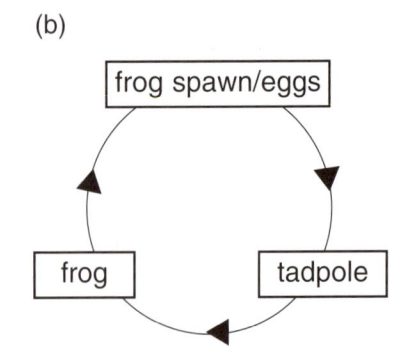

(a) baby → toddler/small child → teenager → adult → (baby)

(b) frog spawn/eggs → tadpole → frog → (frog spawn/eggs)

2 Living things
(a) tobacco (products containing tobacco)
(b) alcohol (drinks containing alcohol / accept illegal drugs e.g. heroin, cannabis, heroin, etc.)

3 Living things
(a) (accept any one of these) micro organisms, mould, bacteria, fungi, microbes
(b) Low temperatures slow down microbe growth – but doesn`t kill them.
(c) Absence/lack of water stops microbe growth.
(d) (i) Heating kills/stops microbe growth.
    (ii) Lack of air kills/stops microbe growth.

4 Materials
(a) It is transparent.
(b) It grips well.
(c) It is strong.

5 Materials
Substance A = solid
Substance B = gas
Substance C = liquid

6 Sound
(a) They move/jump up and down.
(b) They move up and down even more.
(c) It is louder.

7 Forces
(a) He pushes Jack down.
(b) It gets squashed/compressed.
(c) The compressed (squashed) spring pushes up against the lid / the spring exerts force on the lid.

TEST 4
11 x Level 3	5-10 questions correct	working towards Level 3
4 x Level 4	11-14 questions correct	satisfactory Level 3, towards Level 4
10 x Level 5	15-25 questions correct	good Level 4, some Level 5

TEST 5   Level 4 and 5

• Answers to Test 5 •

1   **Living things**

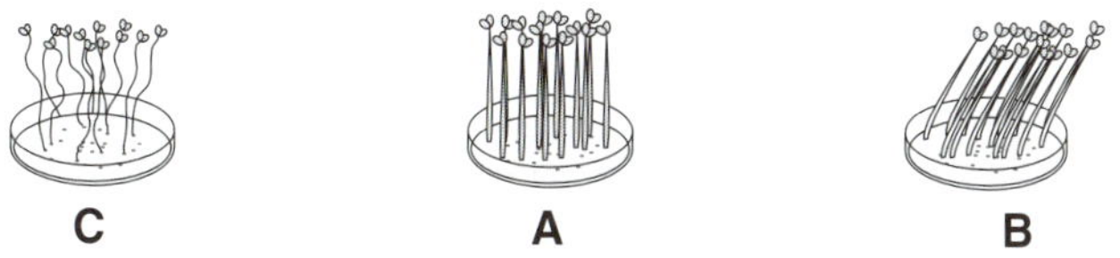

    C   A   B

2   **Living things**
    Walking = 108
    Jogging = 126
    Lying down = 79
    Sitting writing = 89 (numbers pulse beats
    per minute)   *(3 marks)*

3   **Living things**
    (a) fox
    (b) salmon
    (c) newt

4   **Materials**
    (a) by sieving
    (b) They can use a sieve that allows the gravel to pass through, but traps the larger stones.

5   **Materials**
    (a) Plastic is waterproof so prevents the wire from rusting.
    (b) Plastic doesn't conduct electricity so prevents electric shock / short circuits / fire hazards.

6   **Materials**
    (a) by evaporating the water. The salt will be left
    (b) evaporation, then condensation (distillation) / boil the water, collect the steam, cool the steam. Water will be formed/left.

7   **Forces**
    (a) gravity/gravitational force
    (b) Because the force of gravity acting on C is greatest / it has a greater mass
    (c) pull up from string / pull down from gravity
        NB. also accept push up from pan

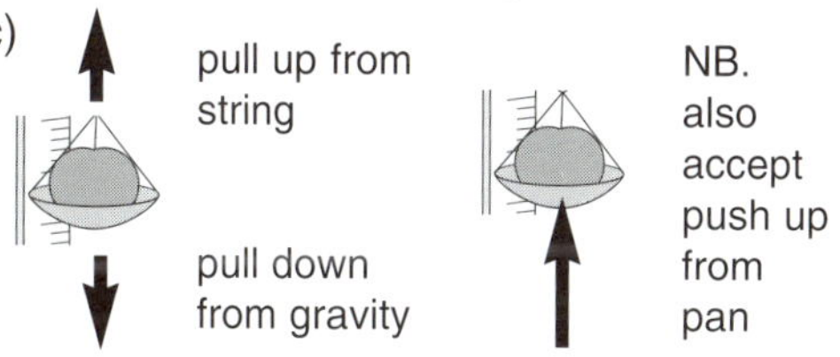

8   **Sound**
    (a) The string vibrates and this makes the air vibrate to produce sound waves/ vibrations. These travel through the air to our ears.
    (b) C
    (c) Use different types of material for 'strings' / use different thicknesses of the same material / put your finger on the string / 'stop' the string.

9   **Forces**
    (a) magnetic force / magnetic attraction
    (b) They move away from the engine.
    (c) Like (similar) poles of a magnet repel/push away from each other.

TEST 5

3 x Level 3	4-11 questions correct	working towards Level 4
12 x Level 4	12-14 questions correct	satisfactory Level 4
10 x Level 5	15-25 questions correct	good Level 4, some Level 5

• 59 •

TEST 6   Level 4 and 5

• Answers to Test 6 •

1 Living things
(a) (i) carry oxygenated blood (or blood containing oxygen) around the body.
(a) (ii) carry deoxygenated blood (or blood containing carbon dioxide) from the body to the heart.
(b) Carbon dioxide passes from the blood into the lungs. Oxygen passes from lungs into the blood. (Carbon dioxide and oxygen are exchanged.)

2 Living things
(a) (i) the skull (ii) the ribs
(b) joints
(c) muscles

3 Living things
(a) weed → snail → starling → fox
    (must be in this order)
(b) (i) weed (ii) snail/starling/fox
(c) There wouldn't be as many / they would fly to another field.

4 Materials
(a) temperature after one hour
    Bottle A = 42°c   Bottle C = 25°c
    Bottle B = 20°c   Bottle D = 56°c   *(4 marks)*
(b) foam rubber
(c) because the hot water stayed the warmest / the foam rubber is the best insulator.

5 Electricity
(a) (iii) – it becomes dimmer
(b) (i) – it becomes brighter

6 Sun and light
(a) [X marked in box]
(b) The earth is spinning (around its axis) and the sun stays in the same place.

7 Sun and light
Arrows must show
• light travelling from light bulb to drawing and
• reflecting off the paper into her eyes.

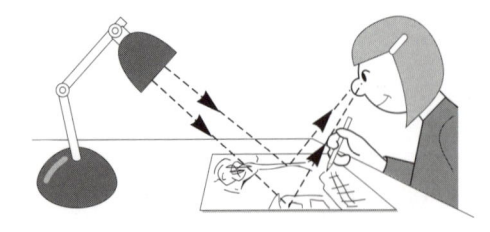

8 Forces
(a) [diagram with arrows]
(b) because the two forces are equal/balanced

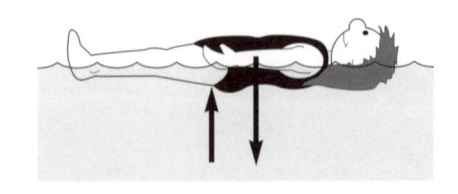

TEST 6		
	6-8 questions correct	working towards Level 4
12 x Level 4	9-11 questions correct	satisfactory Level 4
13 x Level 5	12-25 questions correct	good Level 4, some Level 5

TEST 7   Level 5 and 6

• Answers to Test 7 •

1 **Living things**
   (a) anchors the plant in the ground / stops it blowing over
   (b) absorbs water/minerals/nutrients from the soil

2 **Living things**
   Label A: cell membrane
   Label B: mitochondrion
   Label C: nucleus
   Label D: chromosomes
   Label E: cytoplasm
   (5 marks)

3 **Living things**
   (a) It is dark / no bright sunlight.
   (b) It is damp / their bodies won`t dry up in the sun.
   (c) They are safe from enemies/predators. (OR) It is cool. (accept 3 of 4)

4 **Living things**
   (a) (i) freezing
       (ii) drying
   (b) to prevent germs/bacteria/microbes/fungi in the air coming in contact with food/ to keep it clean.

5 **Materials**
   (a) (i) solid (ii) liquid (iii) gas
   (b) The water vapour (steam) cools as it comes into contact with the glass. As it cools, drops of water are formed. The steam condenses. Condensation takes place. (All of this answer is required to achieve 1 mark.)

6 **Sound**
   (a) (i) Sound waves travel through water.
   (ii) Sound waves are reflected from the object back to the ship.

   (b) [diagram of ship with Sender and Receiver, sound waves traveling to object on seabed]

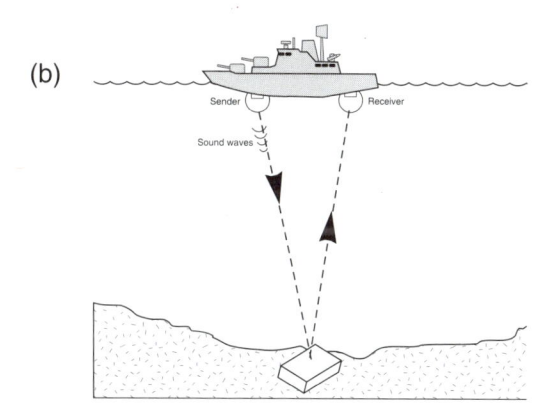

7 **Electricity**
   (a) The wire wool doesn't conduct electricity as well as the wire / The electricity is shared between the light bulb and wire wool / The wire wool has a greater resistance than wire. (Any one of these answers.)
   (b) It was dimmer.

8 **Sun and light**
   (a) (i) [diagram of Sun with Earth and Moon orbiting]
       (ii) 14 days / 2 weeks
   (b) It causes the hours of daylight and darkness in a day to vary throughout the year.

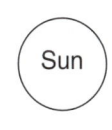

TEST 7

	8-12 questions correct	working towards Level 5
17 x Level 5	13-16 questions correct	satisfactory Level 5
8 x Level 6	17-25 questions correct	good Level 5, some Level 6

TESTS 1 to 4   LEVELS 3 to 5

• Science National Curriculum Record •

	Level 3			Level 4				Level 3			Level 4			Level 5		
	Life processes	Materials	Physical processes	Life processes	Materials	Physical processes		Life processes	Materials	Physical processes	Life processes	Materials	Physical processes	Life processes	Materials	Physical processes
TEST 1							**TEST 3**									
1a				■			1a							■		
1b				■			1b							■		
2a				■			1c							■		
2b				■			1•									
2c				■			2a	■								
2d				■			2b	■								
3•	■						3•	■								
3•	■						3•	■								
3•	■						3•	■								
3•	■						4•				■					
3•	■						4•				■					
4•		■					5a								■	
4•		■					5•								■	
4•		■					5•								■	
4•		■					5•								■	
4•		■					5b								■	
5a					■		6a						■			
5b(i)					■		6b						■			
5b(ii)					■		7a		■							
6a			■				7b		■							
6b			■				8a						■			
7a			■				8b						■			
7b			■				8c						■			
8a			■				8d						■			
8b			■				8e						■			
TEST 2							**TEST 4**									
1•				■			1a	■								
1•				■			1•	■								
1•				■			1•	■								
1•				■			1b	■								
2a(i)				■			1•	■								
2a(ii)				■			1•	■								
2b				■			2a							■		
3a	■						2b							■		
3b	■						3a							■		
3c	■						3b							■		
4•		■					3c							■		
4•		■					3d(i)							■		
4•		■					3d(ii)							■		
4•		■					4a		■							
4•		■					4b		■							
5a			■				4c		■							
5b							5•					■				
6a					■		5•					■				
6b					■		5•					■				
6c			■				6a									■
6d			■				6b									■
7a						■	6c									■
7b						■	7a		■							
8a			■				7b									
8b			■				7c						■			

• 62 •

TESTS 5 to 7   LEVELS 3 to 6

• Science National Curriculum Record •

	Level 3			Level 4			Level 5				Level 5			Level 6		
	Life processes	Materials	Physical processes	Life processes	Materials	Physical processes	Life processes	Materials	Physical processes		Life processes	Materials	Physical processes	Life processes	Materials	Physical processes
TEST 5										**TEST 7**						
1•	■									1a	■					
1•	■									1b	■					
1•										2•						■
2•							■			2•						■
2•							■			2•						■
2•							■			2•						■
3a				■						2•						■
3b				■						3a	■					
3c				■						3b	■					
4a					■					3c	■					
4b					■					4•			■			
5a								■		4•			■			
5b								■		4•			■			
6a										5a(i)		■				
6b										5a(ii)		■				
7a						■				5a(iii)		■				
7b						■				5b		■				
7c						■				6a(i)						■
7•						■				6a(ii)						■
8a									■	6b						■
8b									■	7a			■			
8c									■	7b			■			
9a					■					8a(i)			■			
9b					■					8a(ii)			■			
9c					■					8b			■			
TEST 6																
1a(i)							■									
1a(ii)							■									
1b							■									
2a(i)							■									
2a(ii)							■									
2b							■									
2c							■									
3a				■												
3b(i)				■												
3b(ii)				■												
3c																
4a					■											
4•					■											
4•					■											
4•					■											
4b																
4c																
5a																
5b																
6a						■										
6b																
7									■							
8a																
8a																
8b									■							

Using this Record

Look at the answers for each of the tests. If the answer is wrong, put a cross in the red box beside the question number.

Look at where the crosses are and see where help is most needed in National Curriculum science – and at what Level.

Pupil achievement record

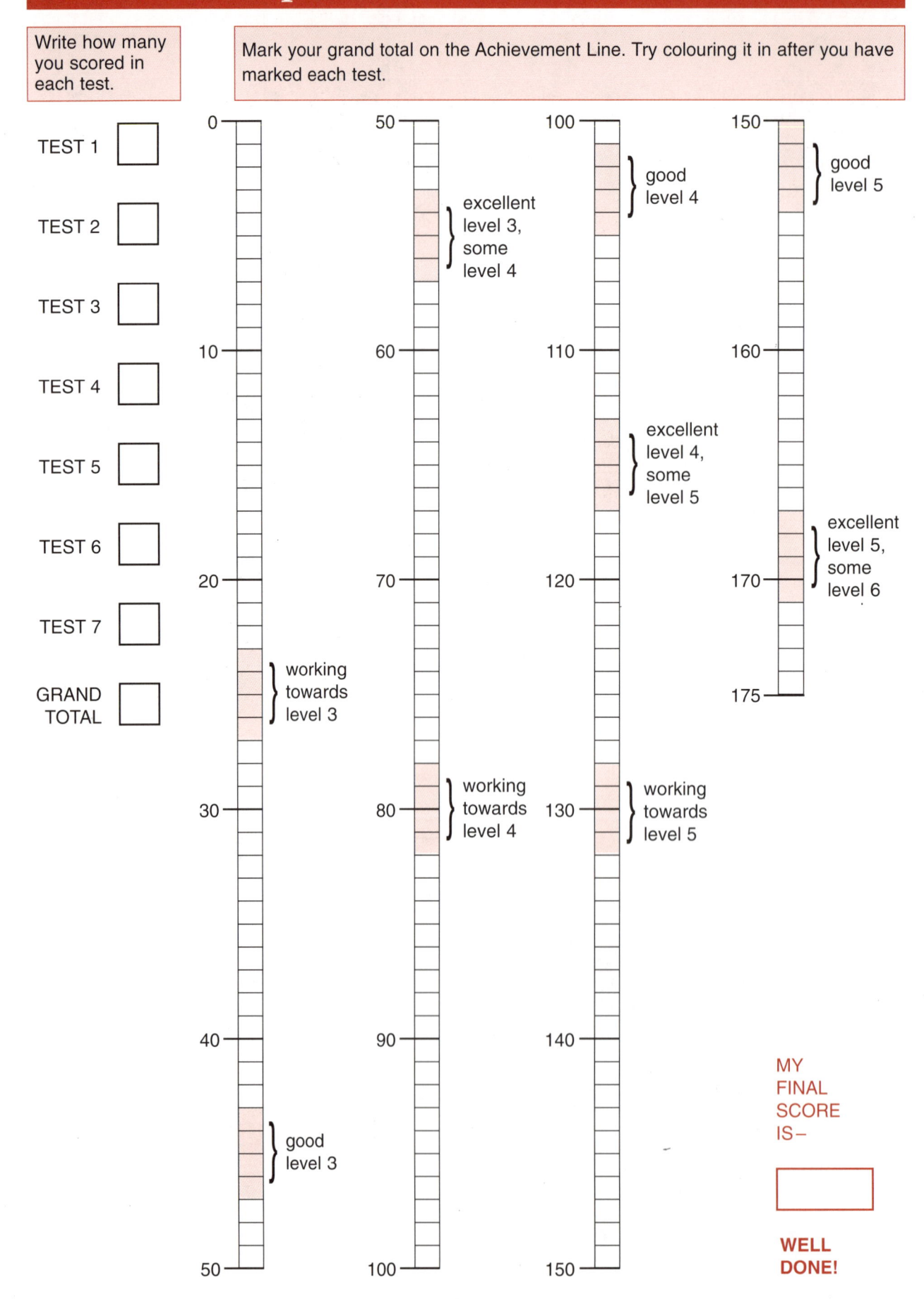

Write how many you scored in each test.

TEST 1 ☐
TEST 2 ☐
TEST 3 ☐
TEST 4 ☐
TEST 5 ☐
TEST 6 ☐
TEST 7 ☐
GRAND TOTAL ☐

Mark your grand total on the Achievement Line. Try colouring it in after you have marked each test.

- } working towards level 3
- } good level 3
- } excellent level 3, some level 4
- } working towards level 4
- } good level 4
- } excellent level 4, some level 5
- } working towards level 5
- } good level 5
- } excellent level 5, some level 6

MY FINAL SCORE IS –

☐

WELL DONE!